Presented to:

_____

Date:

_____

with thanks

To Lesa McCann —
May God Bless

Joe

Amazing Grace

God's provision during widowhood

AMAZING GRACE
God's provision during widowhood
by Jane C. Wittbold

Published by:
RPJ & COMPANY, INC.
P.O. Box 160243 ǀ Altamonte Springs, Florida 32716-0243 ǀ 407.551.0734
Web site: www.rpjandco.com

Copyright © 2011 by Jane C. Wittbold

ISBN-13: 978-0-9829277-2-7
ISBN-10: 0-9828277-2-5

Library of Congress Control Number: 2011922488

Cover & Interior Design by:
RPJ & COMPANY, INC.
www.rpjandco.com

Cover photography:
flower © Andriy Solovyov - Fotolia.com

Scripture verses are quoted from the King James Version of the Bible.
Used by permission. All rights reserved.

Printed in the United States of America.

In memory of my husband
William John Wittbold,
When once he met the Lord,
He gave his love and life to Him.
1927 to 1991

In remembrance of the
Lord Jesus, the anointed One,
the Christ of God,
Who when He became my husband,
Grasped my hand,
and lead me into the future.
ETERNITY

Published by:

RPJ & Company, Inc.
www.rpjandco.com

Amazing Grace

God's provision during widowhood

Table of Contents

PREFACE

There it was. The sign that said "Alligator Alley". The name conjured up all kinds of ancient mysteries and folklore. There was a time when I would have been excited with the prospect of crossing South Florida by this high speed roadway. There was a time I would have enjoyed vacationing at Marco Island, Florida. There was a time it would have thrilled me.

It was a beautifully clear and sunny day, and the traffic was light. Once I would have been irresistibly tempted to push the accelerator to the floor. Once I would have jumped at the chance to test the power of the low white sport coupe I was driving. Once I would have looked forward to the days ahead.

But now, I brushed back my tears and struggled with the short strings of my life. A life once orderly was now an unraveled mess. I needed some time alone, without pressure. I needed to hear from God. Friends had kindly offered their vacation home for a time of isolation and prayer. I needed both. I knew that God would meet me and give me new direction for my life. I felt unsure because I really didn't want a new direction. My life seemed over, but God kept making promises. I felt finished, weary and broken. Life without Bill was just too hard!

Bill had been gone over two years. Since his death I continued to work - to minister and to manage the affairs of the ministry. On the outside I looked OK, but inside there was a raging struggle for my life. It became harder to cope with my emotions. My protection was worn thin. Feelings I thought I had dealt with would suddenly rise up before me like giants and threaten my very sanity.

Life without Bill was an anguish I could no longer bear. It was ripping and tearing at my soul causing terrible pain. Every day I fought to bring my emotions under the authority of the blood of Jesus. Every day was a struggle just to continue the work of the Ministry.

God had given us a miracle in the summer of 1982. That was the first time that my husband, an alcoholic, had come to the point of death. We had little interest in God but during that summer we came to know Him and turned our lives over to Him. After three years of His redemptive work in us, He led us to open ...*in the Name of Jesus Ministries Inc.* in Cocoa Beach, Florida. We had joined together with God and He gave us His wisdom and power. We ministered to all those who came: alcoholics, drug addicts, homosexuals, rapists, adulterers, murderers, anyone in trouble who crossed our threshold. Day and night we met with the hurting children of God. Those who knew Him and those who did not. We were a team and this was definitely a team effort.

But now I was alone and expected to continue as if nothing had happened. The burden was just too great, even with the help of God. So much needed to be done, so many people, so much trouble. It was too large for me to carry. I was only one woman and I was broken at best. The job was too big and everything was just too painful.

I was in this frame of mind when I took the kind offer of this Marco Island house. It was a hiding place where I might quiet my spirit and hear God. It seemed strange to go to a place which Bill would have loved and to go there without him. I cried often on the way down but tears had become my constant companion. It was my first trip alone without Bill. Following my friends' directions I soon turned into their driveway and parked the car. A small white butterfly led me up the stairs to the living quarters.

This was a typical Marco Island house, built high above possible flood tides. It offered marvelous views from every window: canals, tree tops, birds in flight, the Gulf of Mexico. It was a fisherman's paradise. Bill, who had been a fisherman, was in heaven. I, who didn't care, was here. Another imponderable!

I put my suitcases in the bedroom and walked through the house. I was looking for the place where the Lord would meet me and renew me. High above my surroundings I found the room. It was an upper room, made of glass, where I could make my confessions and the power of God would minister to me. It was a special place, a holy place, where I would come to understand what God was doing with my life. I knew each life held purpose, but what was mine? With questions still unanswered I lay down that night to a troubled sleep.

I was awakened before dawn with the sound of distant thunder. I saw the quick white light which betrayed the approaching storm. I threw off the bed covers and made my way up the circular stairs to the upper room. I wanted to see the storm roll in from the Gulf of Mexico. The Lord had often taught me great truths in nature. I felt His encouraging hand as I found my way in the dark. The sun was just beginning to color the clouds and proclaim its role as "ruler of the day."

If I sat pressed into the corner of the room, I could see the entire drama. To my right, the sun bringing light to the darkened world, to my left, the dark turbulence of the awesome storm at sea. Lightning flashing its cold light on one side and the sun bringing its warm life-giving light on the other. I was stuck in the middle, caught up in the awesomeness of God and His creation, but unable to discern which way to look.

The storm was raging and seemed out of control, much like the forces which were driving my life. The sunrise, however, promised a new day. God had been promising me such a new day. He took every opportunity to show me that there was something new ahead. Which way did He want me to look? To the storm or to the new day? As I looked to the new day, I felt His correction forcing me to look into the face of the raging storm. It was dark and turbulent, a churning force, folding and unfolding terribly before me. Dreadfully black and sinister, it seemed determined to cover the whole world in darkness; but with brilliant flashes of jagged lightning, it revealed itself over and over. Nothing else moved. It was hard to breathe as the storm turned upon itself, suffocating the rest of creation. Power, greater than anything I had ever seen, was arrayed before me. Darkness swiftly blacked out the horizon.

Then, there it was. Yes, the storm was overpowering, but as the first few rays of the rising sun made contact with the darkness, His great Promise burst through. A perfect rainbow. It was new and unused with both ends visible. It was brilliant in color, not yet faded by time. Shining and bright against the darkness of the early morning storm. It radiated the ancient promise of God (Genesis 9:12). His promise not to forget His children. His word clearly states that no storm nor flood would overtake us. The rainbow is His sign, His sign to mankind that He is with us forever, no matter our situation or peril. God is faithful to His word. He had allowed the storms to come against me and the darkness to fill my soul. Difficult yes, trying yes, but God had never left me.

Quickly the storm outside was changing. The bow was gone and the blackness blotted out the sun. I could no longer see the new day, but the promise lingered. The memory of that now-hidden sign burned fresh in my mind. I realized anew that God was more powerful than all the evil that had come against me; in truth Bill was with Him but my life was to be made new.

God's plan for my life was not finished. There was to be a new beginning. God would heal me and out of the victory over my pain and heartache would come this book. A work done for God and for those who choose to read it. The story is mine, with Bill and without him. To those dear souls who helped me brave the storms, I say a heartfelt thanks. To those who might read these pages, I pray that you will be blessed and helped by this book. I pray that you, too, will begin to look for the signs that He will give you directing you out of the storm, however dark.

This is a story about hope. If widowhood is your companion and your life seems to be in turmoil, I pray this work will show you that hope is available. I encourage you to look to God and let Him guide you through the dreadful days of your present situation.

May the reading of this book give you peace and bring forth unspeakable joy from any sorrows in your life.

Jane C. Wittbold
Marco Island, Florida

ACKNOWLEDGMENTS

It would be impossible to complete this work without a word of thanks to God who required this book from me, and then proceeded to orchestrate its outcome.

Also, I thank the prophet Jeremiah, who in the 49th chapter, 11th verse of his book made note that the Lord had said, *"and let thy widows trust in me."* This became my true slogan.

And for those who came alongside to help uphold the work at ...*in the Name of Jesus Ministries* in Cocoa Beach, Florida – my heartfelt thanks. For Hollie O'Brien and the home church that met on Wednesday evenings, for Jimmy Smith and the Friday night Fellowship of the Lamb, and for Mel and Brenda Hinton leading the Sunday night meeting. For those who came and upheld the Alcoholics group on Tuesday night and for all those who came to help feed the hungry on Saturday night which was a true work of the home group, Hollie, Hazel, Dorothy, Bette, Phyllis, Ginny, Julie and Bill, who are now in heaven, Lester, Kim, David, Juanita and Jeff, and the many others that came to help.

I also want to thank the Fazio family who truly understood and accepted the responsibility of, "Pure and undefiled religion".

I am most grateful for the help and encouragement given by Laura Watson. I don't think I would have finished without her help. I also must give credit and thanks to my new daughter in Christ, Kathleen Schubitz, whose gifts and talents have helped with the final editing and publishing of this book.

My most special thanks to my wonderful family for patiently awaiting upon my return from the dead. And for my grandchildren who taught me how to use this computer thereby bringing me into the 20th century just as it comes to a close.

My heartfelt thanks to everyone else who found a way to touch my life during these – my worst years. I am unable to mention you all, but just know that all of you took part in my healing and deliverance from grief. For those of you that helped me move, Lester, Kim and Rich, you have my blessings. I also want to thank Janine and Jim and all those who helped create a beautiful atmosphere at the ministry for Bill's memorial. The list goes on but the space is short. My love and eternal thanks to Marilyn, Lojuan, and Carolyn, to Judy, Becky and Stephanie, to Elsa and Essie, to Zoe, and to Terry and Jim and their wonderful children. To Sandi and Joe for the use of their marvelous cottage. And to Mark who stepped in to help lift the burden, but instead has become the servant in that same dread spot.

For those of you who thought of me, and prayed for me, I will be forever grateful. May God bless you abundantly!

Amazing Grace

God's provision during widowhood

JANE C. WITTBOLD

chapter 1

Emergency Room Number 1

Precious in the sight of the Lord is
the death of His saints.
(Psalm 116:15)

 Bill was dead. There was no sign of life in his body. He lay so still on that cold steel table. He gave no sigh of recognition! He was dead, separated from me. He was no longer mine. He had been a big man, a much misunderstood man, but one who had made a difference in people's lives. Now there was nothing. I stood there looking at him, not comprehending. I was seeing but I was not believing. Moments ago he had been alive. He was my husband, my beloved, but now he was dead. He had gone into eternity without a glance back to me. No last farewells, no kisses, not even a wave of his hand. He had gone to God, to heaven, that place we used to talk about, but he had gone without me. We were to go together into death. As we had faced life, we would face death.

We had been married for over forty years, and broken because of the sin in our lives. God met us and joined us by the fire of affliction. We were forged together like hardened steel. We were a team. We had been broken by sin and honed by God. He lead us and we were brought to that place of burning by His Holy Spirit. The dross of our lives burned away through the process of the daily giving of ourselves in ministry. We were His team in the work. Jesus was the head and we were His lesser partners. We were made whole by the Spirit of God. Bill was complete in me and I complete in him. So how could this be happening? This was all wrong! I could see it with my eyes but I could not accept what I was seeing.

Bill had beaten death before; this was to have been the third occasion. The first time was in July of 1982, when God had done a great miracle and brought life out of certain death. Once again in July of 1990, God intervened and spared his life. Now it was July of 1991, and I was sure that this struggle would be like the others, ending victoriously.

Just weeks before, Bill had gone into the hospital. We needed to find out what was wrong. He was tired and experiencing abdominal discomfort. A quick check-up might answer his nagging questions. The three days in the hospital were wonderful for him. Almost everyone came to see him. If the hospital had tried to limit the number of visiting friends, they would have been hard pressed to keep up with the crowd. It was amazing.

Both of our children lived nearby, so they were able to come and spend time with him. There was no way for us to know that these would be their last times together.

The physicians were having a confusing time isolating the exact cause of Bill's discomfort. Kidney stones, sugar diabetes, liver dysfunction, all investigated but cast aside. There seemed no clear answer. Many years before, Bill had been an alcoholic and he had severely punished his body. God had miraculously saved him and set him free from alcohol, giving him an abundant and useful life.

The days in the hospital passed with tests and x-rays, only to lead to more tests and x-rays. No conclusive evidence could be found. They wanted to do one more test, an MRI. We surmised they were looking for liver cancer. Nine years ago Bill's liver had been severely damaged. It had solidified and was unable to function, but God had done a miracle in our lives. We were often asked, "Did God give Bill a new liver, or is He making the damaged one work?" Bill would shrug his shoulders, "What difference does it make. It's working!" He would say it with a smile.

Now with the specter of new and even more expensive tests looming over his head, he wanted to go home. We prayed together and felt the encouragement of the Lord that nothing more could be accomplished in the hospital, so we headed home. I took the phone off the hook and only called the children, or those who needed to know. I gave twice daily reports, strongly believing in my heart that he would be healed. Once again, God would come to our rescue and we would be able to continue with our lives.

We spent our time together talking, praying, crying and remembering. My job seemed to be one of encouragement, to lift his spirits. Bill tried to respond to me in a positive way but he was really so very tired. I asked him once, "Why am I doing all the fighting?" He just looked at me and smiled. His eyes, usually so expressive, were weary. Food tasted terrible to him and he had a poor appetite. I pureed the foods he liked, but it was of no. use. He would try but had little interest or hunger.

My birthday was to be the last day we shared together in the family room. The next day he kept to himself in the bedroom. He tried to find comfort, but was not able. The members of our home church came by to pray for him. He was glad to see them but he seemed unsettled. He slept fitfully. He wanted the room darkened, consequently I was unable to see his skin grow even more yellow.

He spent his last night at home, sleeplessly turning on our bed. My prayers seemed to disturb him so I stayed down the hall, keeping a vigil over him.

In the morning he said, "It's time. Please call for the ambulance." His breathing had become more labored. God gave us confirmation through the timely arrival of our friend who agreed with us, by the Spirit, that it was time to call 911.

Little did I think, as the paramedics took him out of our home, that he would not be back. Even though I felt the Lord take the burden of his care from me and my knees became so weak that I could not stand, I was still believing that God would do another miracle. Weeks before, during a time of prayer, God had clearly given me a scripture to stand on. He had given me John 17:15, *"I pray not that thou shouldest take them out of the world, but that thou shouldest keep them from the evil."* Nothing on this earth could be more powerful than coming into agreement with the Lord, in His own prayer for His disciples. Certainly nothing could stand against that. I gave that scripture to those around me whose prayers I trusted. I was believing and I was expecting them to believe with me.

As the last great drama of Bill's life was being played out, God showed me His provision. Hollie O'Brien, our home church pastor, arrived at the house just as they were taking Bill to the hospital. Another close friend hurried in as I was calling the children to tell them about Dad's return to the hospital. By the time we got to the hospital, we were joined by many faithful friends. They had come to pray with me. Six good women, noble women of God, had closed ranks around me. There we were, seven, to stand in faith for my husband's life. I felt that only good could come of this.

It seemed only a few minutes had passed when the doctors brought the news. I was certainly not prepared. I thought they had come to encourage me, but that was not so. They came to tell me that Bill had succumbed. He was deceased.

"Oh no!" filled my mouth, "You have the wrong man," I said over and over. I shook my head in disbelief. "My husband will live and declare the works of the Lord!" I continued to shake my head, "You have the wrong man," I said it over and over. The doctors were very kind but very insistent. Bill was gone, if I would wait a few minutes while they prepared his body, they would let me see him.

Obediently my feet moved, my body did all it was called to do. However, an overwhelming numbness took possession of my mind and my heart. I dreaded going into that room. I was not ready to believe the doctors' report, yet I was anxious to see Bill. They couldn't dismiss him like this. He was a child of God, an overcomer.

I shuddered as I entered this death room. Everything was in absolute stillness, not a sound. The life-giving machines were quiet, no longer needed. The room was strange and foreign. This was not a room that Bill would have liked. I quickly looked at his body. All the life was drained out of him. I could not accept what I was seeing, this could not be so. This was just a cruel trick. It was a mistake, a bad dream, a nightmare, but certainly not the truth.

Soon it was obvious that his body no longer functioned. Breath was gone from him. That breath that God had breathed into him was gone. That distinctive yellow cast on those who suffer from liver disease, not as noticeable at home, was very evident here. I could see clearly under the harsh, bright, unforgiving lights of this medically-correct death room.

Everything in the room was so cold and sterile, so impersonal. It was such a foreign place, a place in which I was not free. I was not free to take hold of him and clasp him to me and breathe my life into him.

There were medical people standing around, and the six who had come together to pray. There was no privacy, no moment alone with him. I needed to be alone now, to yell out to God, to cry, maybe to join him in death; but that was not to be.

We stood at the cold steel gray table where his body lay. I could see clearly, painfully, that his body was at rest. The dark circles now muted under his eyes, a peaceful smile on his lips, his face was beautiful. His heart had been beating when the medics had taken him out of the house. Now it was forever still. There was not even a telltale twitching of an eyelash to betray a secret life within him. There was nothing now. No movement, no heartbeat, nothing. Just the jaundiced body of my beloved, dead in this world, but alive in the next.

Oh, God, how could you do this? We were a team. Together we functioned, together we worked, together we laughed and loved. Now I stood beside him, helplessly. I could not change anything. God had taken it out of my hands. I just stood there, not believing the scene which lay before me.

One in our midst reached out her hands, laid them on him and called his spirit back. So many times we read about the Lord, filled with the power of God, calling back the spirits of the dead. However, in this case nothing happened, and I knew nothing was going to happen.

Though I stood in the company of those who loved us, I was hearing from a different realm. I was clearly hearing angelic voices. A choir, singing in the midst of that great circle of witnesses, welcoming Bill home. A beautiful song drifted down into my spirit, filling me with its silvery sound and its golden message. I heard them proclaiming Bill's "rite of passage," as they sang the words that I will never forget: "Broken and spilled out in the service of the Lord." That sweet refrain came over and over again, reaching notes that only angels could sing. The music and the message were harmoniously woven together into a beautiful anthem. I heard the heavenly beings welcome Bill, and he joined together with them. He was eagerly anticipating that which lay ahead, always curious, always interested. This great inquisitive man was now happily pressing forward to meet his God.

I was surrounded by friends but very much alone as I spoke the painful words, "I release you to a loving God and into His Hands I commit your spirit."

That was the first time that I would speak such words. But as time went on, I would speak them again and again as I let go of Bill little by little, and memory by memory.

chapter 2

R͟EꞮꞱ UR͟NING H͟OME

The LORD was as an enemy: he hath swallowed up Israel,
he hath swallowed up all her palaces:
he hath destroyed his strong holds,
and hath increased in the daughter of Judah
mourning and lamentation.
(Lamentations 2:5)

 Bill's miraculous life was over. He and I had lived in the midst of a special gift from God. We had walked together in the Spirit and now it was time for me to turn and walk away, alone.

I left the earthly remains of my husband and walked out of that dreadful room, Emergency Room Number 1. I hoped never to see that place again. Mechanically I took care of the legalities and details regarding the disposition of my beloved. Since it was Saturday, the hospital would keep his body for the autopsy which would be performed on Monday. I signed some papers and joined the others.

A time before, I had driven my friend, a new widow, home in a similar situation from another hospital. Her first husband had gone on to be with God. Now life held an unreal quality as I climbed into the car next to her and she prepared to drive me home.

I vaguely remember asking her, "Is this why we are called the Bride of Christ? Will the end of the church age be made up of widows and spinsters?" To the casual observer our drive home might have seemed calm and uneventful, but my mind was in a raging turmoil. What do I do now? Where do I begin? What happened? Where did I miss God? What went wrong? Where are you, Bill? Don't leave me, Bill! Please come back to me! Bill, Bill, Bill, I can't make it without you.

The children! I must call Katherine and John. Had I misled them? Standing in faith for life is difficult, but by doing so, had I robbed them from being with Bill in death? We live life trying to protect our children, but had I gone too far? Would they resent me? The Lord had painstakingly rebuilt our relationships. My reaction to the years of Bill's alcoholism had destroyed much between us. Would that which God had built stand now, or was it all too fragile, I wondered.

I dreaded making those phone calls. I had, just a few hours before, told them that Daddy would be OK, that the ambulance had come to take him to the hospital. Now I was telling them that he was dead. How is this all possible? Bill had come through worse situations. God had saved him from death before. Why not now? I prayed,

"Please God, make me understand so that I can help them understand. Please Lord, help me do things in the proper order." God was order. Would He share His order with me now, I wondered. There was so much to do and I was so confused. My mind was in a disarray. It was as if the ache in my heart had finally mastered my mind and I could no longer think clearly.

What would the future hold? Did I really hear the voice of God? Why did the Holy Spirit lead me to have faith for healing, when He knew that God would take Bill home? One question after another wheeled through my mind. They weighed me down and caused distraction.

I must restore order to the house. Things would need to be changed, medicines put away. Our bed would need making, rooms needed dusting, bathrooms needed cleaning. I thought of food, we had none. Bill had been on homemade baby food and I had been fasting. People would be coming and I needed to feed them. The pain had finally won and confusion reigned within me.

Grace under fire. I had heard the term used in humor and in conflict, now I was in it. God did order my steps. It is an amazing experience, walking in the Grace of God. My emotional state was raw and turbulent, but my spirit was at peace when I sat at Bill's desk and prepared to call the children. Katherine was home. I had talked to her earlier when I offered hope, but had been giving her the worst possible news. "Honey, Daddy is gone. He died. He went to be with God." I really don't remember all of our conversation. I only remember that I tried to comfort her. She offered to come but I felt she needed to be with her family. I told her not to come, that I would see her later, somehow. She understood. We both needed time to sort out our emotions. I needed time to lay before God. I needed to hear His voice. I needed His answers to my many questions. I needed to feel His comforting presence, however, later it was taken out of my hands when one in the group phoned Katherine and suggested that she should come. So she was coming, coming to be with me. "Bless her Lord, protect her as she comes. Hold her close to you. Please Lord, she loved her Daddy so very much. This will be very hard for her." She was our firstborn and held that special place in our hearts.

The call to John, our only son, left me unsettled. John had been a bright and sensitive child. He had grown into a gentle man with a great inner conflict. He was our youngest, a very special child in every way. Of the two children, he had been the most touched by Bill's drinking. I had not been able to reach him when I left the earlier message. Again I was confronted by his answering machine. I didn't know what to do, but I did know that I had to be the one to tell him. News of this sort travels so fast, and I was concerned that he might hear this dreadful truth from some other source. I left the message on his answering machine. Many times since, I have wondered, how could I have left such a message on his machine? How could I just blurt out that

Daddy was gone? In retrospect, it was possibly easier for John to be alone when he heard the message. God had given him time to deal with the early shock before he was forced to face everything that lay ahead.

Both of our children were important to us and we loved them dearly. They were as different as night is from day, but we appreciated the differences. They were never far from our hearts.

They had not truly understood what had happened to us in that dramatic summer of 1982. We had become born again by the Grace of Almighty God, and our lives were forever-changed. The children were forbearing if not wholeheartedly in agreement with us. Though they did not understand, they could not deny the great and mighty changes that had taken place in our lives. We had not raised them in a Christian household, so we could expect nothing else but their doubtful acceptance. They were glad for us and it kept Daddy sober, so they did nothing to interfere with our new lifestyle. We were aware, however, that the changes in us had caused them some uncomfortable moments.

But now, I was telling them that I had been wrong, as far as Daddy's condition went. Daddy was not OK! This time God hadn't touched Bill to heal him. In fact He had taken him away, far away from us who loved him. I prayed a quick, though silent prayer, "Oh God, help me to understand that which you have done. Make me able to show the children the truth. Help me behave as if I believe the truth."

The worldly things were out of my hands. Those who had stood with me in the hospital had been making arrangements. People started arriving. Our wonderful friend and lawyer came loaded down with food. Others were in the kitchen, setting things in order and taking charge of the telephone.

Food was prepared and set out. People kept coming through the front door with offers of help. Some very special friends even tackled the yard, which had been neglected in sacrifice to Bill's final illness. They cut the grass, trimmed the bushes and cut back the banana leaves. I will always remember, in gratitude, their sorrowing faces glistening with sweat as they did what was before them to do. Soon the rest of those who had stood with me in the hospital were there. Others came and went. Friends, neighbors, acquaintances, the callers came one after the other. There were so many and I can't recall them all. They came in love to offer help. Aside from a touch and a prayer there was precious little more that they could do. I was beyond human help!

Then Bill's secretary arrived. Just weeks before, she had tearfully given us her notice. Her husband was being transferred by his company. It was a good promotion, but it meant leaving the area. She stood at the door, looking at me with tears spilling from her eyes. She stamped her little foot saying, "I at least gave him my two weeks' notice."

We held onto each other for a long time. She knew what few others knew, that the work was hard. Helpers came and went, but we were the ones who stayed. There was fire in the trenches every day. She also knew how tired Bill had become.

Katherine walked in. She came into the midst of all this commotion. There were people offering their respects, people full of conversation, there were tears, food, and telephones ringing. She walked into a room full of people whom she did not know. She came home to a place changed since her childhood and now never to be the same again, a home without her Daddy. I was thankful to see her no matter the cause for her visit. She was a part of us and I found that I really needed her. I held onto her tearfully with my broken heart spilling its pain.

I really don't remember all that happened after Katherine's arrival. She got busy preparing the obituary while I sought a picture of Bill to add to the copy. We had been politically active. Bill had served a term on the board of trustees of our local community college. He had also been employed at Kennedy Space Center during the great rush to the moon. And he spent years teaching in a college classroom. He had been involved in many things, but none had given him the satisfaction as did ministering to those who were lost and hurting in this troubled world.

I called the undertaker. He said that as soon as the hospital would release his body, they would take care of all the arrangements. Bill was to be cremated. His Christian faith had done nothing to change his mind about that, so I honored his request and gave the instructions to the funeral director. We would be having a memorial service. The time and place had not yet been decided, but we agreed to stay in touch with each other.

Evangelist Jimmy Smith, a good friend and gifted man of God, called to give me comfort. Bill and I had made plans to attend his concert, which would be held the following evening at the Tabernacle Church in Melbourne, Florida. We had worshiped there, at the Tab, for a number of years. Jimmy was giving a fund raising concert to aid his upcoming mission trip to Africa. The Lord had spoken to him and he was to dedicate this concert to Bill's "homegoing". I told him that the family would attend. It had begun! I was making plans without Bill.

I wanted this terrible day to go away. I really wanted to be left alone. I needed to cry, to get before the Lord and ask questions. I wanted my home to myself, so that I might walk its corridors, kick the air, or just lay down and weep. Instead, I sat with those who loved me and began to make plans for the memorial service. It would be held at the ministry building, a date was selected, evening was chosen so that more people could attend. Special speakers were discussed. All the arrangements seemed to fall together in the hands of those who excel in those sorts of things.

More than anything, I wanted time. Time to be alone. There seemed precious little of it available. There was so much to be done. It was a gruesome day and I had a weird feeling that I was somehow suspended between the two great forces of truth: life and death. Bill was dead, but things kept going on. The world did not stop just because I wanted it to. I wanted to talk about Bill, but people just wanted to make plans. My thoughts were of Bill. Everything else was a dark void. My mind was so fragile that it seemed perilously close to breaking. I was being drawn ever closer into the impenetrable vortex of death and I could not judge what lay beyond.

Little by little, those who had come began going away. The tide that had rushed in, knocking down everything in its path, was finally on its way out. The crowd of people gave way to what was left of my family. Katherine, John, his wife, and me. We seemed so few, so inadequate to be left to attend to such great pain. We clung to each other and the memories of Bill, as husband and father. His imprint was still very strong upon us and our home. His recently-purchased medicine bottles stood neatly in a row, his Bible, crossword puzzles, pens, highlighters, all were in easy reach from his overstuffed arm chair and footstool. His place of comfort and study. A place which he no longer needed, just as he no longer needed us. His chair looked disconsolate, and if furniture could express feelings, it would have felt as we did, abandoned and unnecessary. In truth, Bill did not need any of us anymore.

God had not left me, I knew that. The Word said so. Truth told me that I was standing on Jesus, the Rock of my salvation. I must confess though, that I felt like I was mired in quicksand. It was great in its proportion, but shaky and unstable underfoot. I was sinking with every step, into a deeper and deeper despair.

The long night passed. I slept fitfully. Our large bed, once so comforting, was now strange and lonely. Many times I reached out for Bill in the night. He was not there.

chapter 3

JIMMY'S CONCERT

Thou hast turned for me my mourning into dancing:
thou hast put off my sackcloth,
and girded me with gladness;
(Psalm 30:11)

 We awoke before dawn and realized that the air-conditioner was not cooling. It had felt a little warm during the night, but I thought it was caused by the great crowd of people, coming and going through the front door. A repairman came but the needed part would not be available for a few days. We could no longer stay in the house so we quickly attended to the few remaining details and Katherine drove me to her home in Winter Park, Florida.

I knew she was anxious to get home to her family. Her husband had been very generous to let her stay with me for that first night, but a wife belongs with her husband and children. I knew the children would have many questions. I prayed for the correct answers. Bright but sad little faces met the car as Katherine pulled into the driveway. Hugs, tears, kisses, more hugs and tears greeted us. I hated the fact that Bill was not there to see these children.

They were our future, as a people and a nation. So able, quick and vigorous, wise beyond their years, our gifted grandchildren. Katie so tall and slim for ten years, and John Palmer all arms and legs at seven. They represented the future, but it seemed as if I were stuck in the past. They tried to encourage me but they, too, needed encouragement.

I wondered if this was to be my life without Bill, going from place to place like a gypsy, never being rooted in anything. A dried old tumbleweed rolling along at the slightest breeze, falling before the wind and wandering forever. The loneliness and the pain just going on and on, in a never-ending travail before the Lord. I needed to talk with the little ones and tell them that Grandpa was with Jesus. His body was useless to him now but his spirit was with God. He was happy and well. Grandpa was free from this earthly world and had gone into another, a much better world. He would never again be sick or in pain. He would cry no tears. There would be no unhappiness. He would never be disappointed again. He was in a world filled with joy everlasting in the presence of the King. God was all that Grandpa would ever need and He would keep Grandpa safe, waiting for us to join him some day. It was easy to say these words because I believed them. Behaving as though they were true was another matter.

I would often burst into tears, overwhelming me and the children. I never knew what occasion would cause the explosion from within. I was like a cracked dam and I was likely to burst open at any moment. Nothing could stand against my tears. I would leave the table in the middle of a meal to rush outside and weep. I had asked for time to weep, and now the Lord had supplied, but I really wanted to be strong for Katherine and the children.

The grief came by waves, and when it washed over me I became helpless and would seek escape. The family offered comfort and in those first hours with them, I took it. I floundered from Christian strength to questioning the purposes of God. I did not lose my faith in Him, but the shock of Bill's death made me war against the fact that Bill was gone, that he was out of my life, forever.

As the hours passed at Katherine's house, we drew strength from each other. The children drew me closer to them and would gently touch me or offer me their hand. I was dry, and they offered comfort in my desert.

Surprisingly I found no comfort in the Word of God. I would open the Bible to read, but instead I would weep. The words that had been so important to me in the past, now wore a shroud of heaviness. Again and again I would go to the Word only to end in weeping and deep grief. I felt the presence of the Lord and sustained comfort in Him, but I could not read about Him.

Over the years I had learned that if I would allow the grace
of God to flood my heart, then I would hear His voice and
be at peace. Even in the midst of turmoil I could have
God's peace. It was in those special times that direction
would come. I felt that it was OK to set the Bible down for
a while. His Word would come in other ways. After all, I
knew God, I had a personal relationship with Him. I did
not need the printed page as much as I needed Him—His
presence, His touch, and His Spirit.

Bill and I had moved in the supernatural since our
conversion. God's glory and His Spirit had directed us
in times of ministry and in times of great personal stress.
I now felt released from the organized thoughts of God
through men, to trust only in the presence and direction
of His Holy Spirit. If I would allow Him, then He would
lead me and I would function in grace and His peace
could be mine. On those occasions when I would rely on
the natural, the supernatural would not function for me.
When I would realize that I again had taken control, I
would confess my sin and let go of the authority of my life.
Then He would lead me through all the mine fields that lay
ahead. I recalled, with a smile, those times when I would
look in vain for a misplaced object. If in my frustration I
would only stop for a moment, pray, and wait on Him, the
lost object would be quickly found.

Calls were made to family and friends, and calls were
received from family and friends. Plans still demanded
our attention; calls telling of the final preparations for

the memorial service. Bill's brother and his wife would be arriving tomorrow about noon. They were flying down from Michigan, would rent a car and be with us for the service. Calls came in from everywhere. Old friends from our early days before we came to know Christ and from those who had walked with us in Christian faith. I talked with Bill's roommates from our old college days. There were so many people impacted by this last chapter in Bill's life.

The day seemed filled with small pieces of the total drama, each piece containing its own hurts and sorrows. As we dressed, preparing to attend the concert at the church, it seemed as if days had passed since I had told Jimmy that we would be there. In fact, it was just yesterday afternoon.

The family had never been in a charismatic church before. Our son John had attended with us once and we could tell that he thought we were a little bit crazy. We arrived a little early and they let us into the building. For the first time we took our seats as a family. This had been a desire of Bill's heart and mine: the family, saved and worshiping God together. Bill's death had brought us to church together, but I would have to believe God for the rest.

People streamed through the doors of the church; they were anticipating an evening filled with joy. Jimmy's playing and singing could usher listeners into the manifest presence of God faster and more thoroughly than anyone else I have ever heard. He is one of the most anointed public worshipers within the Body of Christ. He was Bill's favorite. I was so pleased when I heard that he had accepted the task of honoring Bill at his upcoming memorial service.

Tonight was special for Jimmy. He had given concerts all over the world but never before in his own church. The auditorium was filled as he came forward, giving the applause to the Lord. He made a few announcements and then he declared that the Lord had told him to dedicate this concert to the home going of Bill Wittbold. The applause was hesitant at first, but as Jimmy encouraged people to express their feelings, it became loud and clear. These were people who knew that the death of a saint was precious to the Lord, and they were pleased to take a place, standing with those who were saying goodbye to Bill. This was to be more than just a concert for me, it was to be a joyous send off. I felt that deeply within my heart. Jimmy called my name, and I stood to receive a perfect white rose which was a gift to me from Jimmy, also at the direction of the Lord.

He played that night like I have never heard him play before. Strong and powerfully, the music poured forth from his hands and voice. Our spirits soared to the throne room of God and I was lost in the reverence of the moment. I saw Bill! He was standing with Jesus, before the throne of God. Bill was celebrating with us and all about him the angels and the holy ones were celebrating. I was lifted out of myself and my pain, into the praises of men and angels. I was grateful in knowing that Bill was in heaven, safe with God. He was no longer burdened by the pull of this earth.

Set free eternally, he was at last in total joy and peace. He was in the kingdom of God, received as a son, a crown on his head, a royal robe around his shoulders. He was dressed all in white with the mark of the blood of Jesus around his hem, in a deep scarlet border. How beautiful he looked! I wanted to be with him, but I could not, so I finally pulled my eyes away.

As I looked at my family they, too, were caught up in the music and I knew that it was helping them. My grandson, John Palmer, was the most visibly touched. He had put his head in Katherine's lap and the tears rolled quietly down his little face. Good music had always affected him but I wondered if he, too, had seen Bill. The evening was wonderful, a good mix of laughter and tears. It was over much too soon.

An amazing thing happened after the concert. With the music still ringing in our ears, the body of Christ came forward. One after the other they came to hug me and speak of their remembrances of Bill. They came wanting to meet his family. It was an overwhelming experience. So many came, some I barely knew, but they came to share some of this very special evening with us. It was very touching. Even Jamie and his wife stood in line to touch our lives. The Buckinghams, as founders and pastors of the Tab, had generously shared their lives with the body through the years, and now in death they came forth to give me comfort.

It was classic Jamie. He was shaking his head as he said, "Here I have been struggling against cancer, preparing to die, and Bill beats me to it." It was true. For a full year Jamie had struggled against death. He shared with his church his symptoms, trials, and fears. Bill and I had sat listening every Sunday to Jamie's saga. Bill, however, without a word, had gone on to be with the Lord.

I heard myself laugh and say to Jamie, "For good or evil, Bill Wittbold was always first in line." I reminded Jamie that if God had not intervened, Bill would have died in 1982. "God gave Bill nine extra years of life," I stated. They hugged me and the line moved on.

This perfect evening came to a close. John and his wife returned to their home in Cocoa while Katherine and the children escorted me to the car for the trip back to Winter Park. It had been another long and difficult day, seasoned with moments of great joy.

Bill had been gone about thirty-six hours and I faced my third night without him. When we arrived at their home, one of them put the rose in a bud vase for me and its fragrance filled the room where I was to sleep.

chapter 4

THE BEGINNING

To every thing there is a season,
and a time to every purpose under the heaven:
(Ecclesiastes 3:1)

We drove along silently, Bill's brother, his wife and I. They had arrived in Orlando just that morning and we were now on our way to Cocoa Beach.

They would stay at the Hilton. We would go together to visit with Aunt Gerry. She was their aunt, Bob and Bill's, and she was a great favorite of us all. She had lived until recently in Palm Beach. Due to circumstances which I will share with you later, she had come to live near us. She was well over 90 and still quite able, but the family was concerned about her. Bill's brother and his wife were looking forward to seeing her, and I was very grateful that they would be there with me, to help tell her about Bill's death.

I rested my head against the seat cushion and stared blankly at the passing scene. We had traveled on this highway many times, Bill and I, good times and bad, but this was definitely the worst. All the plans that we had made, all our hopes and dreams, now gone. In an instant the earth shakes underfoot and one's dreams all crumble. I watched the scenery pass. Blurred by my tears, the once familiar seemed now so strange.

Memories filled my thoughts. I gave traffic directions mechanically saying, "Get into the right lane Bob, you'll want to take the Cape Canaveral, Cocoa Beach road." I paid little attention to the passing scene as my thoughts traveled back to our beginnings. Bill's and mine. How did all of this happen? How did I get to this place? How is it possible that I am riding now with Bill's brother and his wife, but without Bill? He had been so much a part of us; I could not bear the thought that he was gone.

Bill, Bill, Bill. I had been calling on you for years. What went wrong? I remember so long ago when we promised ourselves and each other, that we would not part. "For better or for worse," that's what the minister had said. "Keeping yourselves only for the other." You are supposed to be with me now. I remembered that part of the service clearly. I had forgotten about "till death do us part."

Death had parted us and I felt the separation breaking my heart. I did not choose to be separated from him. He was my Bill, my beloved, my completion. Now there was nothing. Separation! My heart felt as if it had a large hole in it. I could feel the tearing away of the flesh and a great part of me was missing. Though in retrospect, he had left me often. Every time he reached for a gin bottle, he left me. Small, hardly perceptible little separations. Bill and his chosen friend, leaving me behind. So many years had been lost to us.

We had fallen in love while we were still in college. We had dated for a year and then were married. Much of our after-hour college life had been spent in bars, favorite watering holes, where bright young men and women would congregate to let off pressure. It all seemed harmless enough at the beginning, but it set a pattern for us that became a road filled with trouble and pain. Bill was a good student. He had a fine mind and was fun to be with. But far too often, the evening would end badly. With our scholastics completed we moved to Michigan. We set up life in the midst of Bill's family. They were wonderful people and our future seemed secure.

Bill was the first of the three brothers to marry. He was the middle son, Bob was the elder and John, called Bud, was the youngest. I was the first bride and paved the way for the two others to follow. Bill's mom and dad were generous and loving, but after a few months our eyes turned back to Florida. I know we disappointed them but we saw our future elsewhere. Warm and easy, touched by the sun, Florida beckoned and we left Michigan, once again to choose the simpler life in Central Florida.

We were not religious people. In actuality we were non-religious. We had both been "silver spoon babies" and had seldom been deprived of anything. We had never experienced loss, so we lived our lives in an arrogant confidence that the future was owed us and that God was the opiate of those less able. We had a home, children, and Bill's jobs always got better and better. Life was good. Bill was selling building materials, and I was a licensed general contractor. We moved to Brevard County in the late 1950's as the Cape Canaveral Space Center was being built, finally settling in Cocoa Beach.

Brevard County was booming and life was fast and vibrant. The world's most interesting and brilliant people flocked to the area. Though there never was a real sense of permanence, it was an exciting place to live. America was in a race to prove world dominance in outer space. It was thrilling to be part of the adventure. Bill eventually went to work in aerospace and our lives were full. Bill was looking upward while I kept my eyes on the ground. Building was interesting but the greater challenges seemed to be in government. I became a political animal and spent years entranced by the "movers and shakers". Bill and I shared many victories mixed in with a few losses. I really enjoyed those times and it seemed as if we "had it all together".

Man landed on the moon and the great thrill of exploration ended with a whimper. Then the "Space Coast" came under a blanket of pink slips, as the big push ended. Men and women who had worked with their eyes on the sky were suffering their first real unemployment. The face of Brevard County changed drastically. Most people went back to where they came from, but we stayed. Finances were not a real problem in the beginning. Bill's great weakness with alcohol, which had always been with us, was now becoming my paramount concern. He was a smart man with an inquiring mind. Though he had a history of drinking more than was good for him, he had always been able to work. With no evidence of a job, he became easily bored, and he turned away from me, to his other good friend.

Little by little, he drifted further away from me and from the children. Bill and I had always been more than just husband and wife. He had been my best friend and I, his. There was one, however, who was taking an ever larger role as friend, and that was Ethyl Alcohol.

While at the Space Center, Bill had taken advantage of the many opportunities open to those who worked with aerospace companies. He had enrolled in graduate school and had completed his master's degree in business administration. He finally found work, teaching business courses at a local college extension program. He happily arranged his life around the classroom and the bottle.

I, on the other hand, feeling abandoned, had opened a small dress shop for larger ladies. For the very first time our lives took totally separate paths. We still lived together in the same house but the continual erosion of separation, different interests, alcohol and eventual betrayal, caused a mighty fall of all that we had been.

It was the summer of 1982 and our lives were unmanageable. Bill was sick and had finally hospitalized himself. I faced sure bankruptcy — physically, emotionally, and financially. What a deceiving friend alcohol had become. Everything I had ever believed in, people whom I had trusted, every strength that I had ever called upon, had finally failed. We were broken and nonfunctional and our lives were in a dirty disarray. Everything around us fell in shambles. Eventually suicide seemed the only option for me. Bill was in the hospital so he would be taken care of. The children now had their own lives so they would be taken care of. I was the odd man out anyway. Everyone had left me and I was so weary that I couldn't fight anymore.

On the long weekend of the 4th of July, I tried to close the door on my life. At least that was my intent. During Bill's stay in the hospital I had taken to sleeping in his chair. The television had become my comforter. I was encouraged by an employee, the only born again Christian that I knew, to watch Christian programming. She had come to work for us, and we saw something in her that we had never seen before. We used to laugh about it and remarked that if you could ever bottle what our employee had, the world would be a better place.

I was amazed that people really believed in a loving, caring God. One who knew us and wanted a relationship with us. I listened with some unbelief as I heard testimony after testimony on the Christian television station. It all seemed pretty far-fetched to me. I had known church people all of my life, and most of them didn't seem any different from the unchurched. Their church had done precious little to change them. They looked like everyone else. They didn't look as if their heart held something special. Judy was the only one who looked different.

That night in the darkness of the room, with only the prospects of suicide ahead, I called out to Him. "Is it true what they say about you, Jesus?" I wept in anguish, "If it's so, then you had better help me, because I am about to do something very foolish."

That's all it took! In an unmeasurable flash of time, Jesus was there. His presence was all about me, the atmosphere was charged with electricity He held me and comforted me and I lay as a child weeping uncontrollably against His chest. He let me cry it out and then He filled me with His peace.

It was all true! Jesus was real. He was the Son of God and He loved me. God loved me, Jesus loved me, and the Holy Spirit loved me. All night long He filled me with His love. In a moment of time I knew that I was saved. Saved from death, from want, from lack, from harm and a dozen other things. As a new day dawned I drove to the hospital. It was imperative that I go quickly and tell Bill of God's love and to pray with him to receive Jesus in his heart.

Now as if through a fog, Bob interrupted my thoughts and asked, "How far is the Hilton from here?" He had startled me and I shook myself back to the present. We were there, and I pointed to the hotel parking lot. We went up to their rooms so they could change from their travel clothes. I sat waiting on them, but my mind seemed determined to once again find the past.

chapter 5

BORN AGAIN

I had fainted, unless I had believed to see the goodness of the
LORD in the land of the living.
(Psalm 27:13)

M y mind seemed determined to look backward, into the past. I was remembering again the summer of 1982. I could see the hospital room. I could almost smell the heavy sickening antiseptic that hospitals seem to wear, splashed on like some cheap cologne. Bill was so sick, he just lay there feverish and jaundiced from the toxins in his blood, but he seemed eager to pray with me. It must have been a strange scene.

I had known the Lord for only a few hours and here I was, praying with Bill to accept Christ. The only time he had heard the Lord's name coming from my mouth was as a curse, not a blessing. Now I was excitedly telling Bill that Jesus had touched me and I was filled with hope for the future. Our lives were not over, they were really just beginning. If we would slam the door on our past and open the new, even greater door, God would give us a new life.

It would be full to overflowing with His care and His love. Bill received the good news and he too, sick of the old, reached out his hand and prayed with me.

It was all so simple. It seemed almost too simple. All we had to do was trust God! If we would trust Him with everything, He would do the rest. No wonder our lives had become so broken - we had no foundation, no solid rock on which to build. Our house had been built on sand and the fall of it was very great. Now things would be different as we put our lives in the hands of the greatest Builder of them all.

Bill quickly began to improve. He began taking walks around the corridors of the hospital. It was slow at first, but each new day he walked with new strength and confidence. We were able to think a little about the future, even managing to laugh occasionally. God was indeed making changes in our lives. Life looked promising. But as suddenly as things began to improve, disaster struck.

I arrived at the hospital early that morning. As I stepped out of the elevator I heard Bill's voice echoing down the hall. It was loud and he sounded angry. He was yelling frantically and I quickly turned toward his room. I hurried down the hall listening to the sound of his voice, wondering what had happened. The sight that was before me was overwhelming.

He had been put in restraints; both his arms and his legs were tied to the framework of the bed. He lay barely covered, writhing and shouting in a language that I did not recognize. His body would arch and strain as he pulled against the restraints, trying desperately to break their hold on him. He twisted and pulled with the strength of many men, and all the frustration and pain that was in him was coming out in sound. In all the years that I had known Bill, I had never heard him yell in anger. I didn't know if this was anger, or what it was. I didn't know what was happening, but whatever it was he would not stop. He fought, as if caught up by some horrible power and held captive in its mighty grasp. He was trapped, twisting and turning, yelling and screaming. He was being tormented by something and I didn't understand any of it.

How could this be happening? After all weren't we trusting God? What was this that held Bill in its grip? A nurse finally answered my call. She explained to me that during the night Bill's liver had solidified, which put him in a perilous situation. If the liver didn't function then the blood could not be cleansed. The nurse said that the condition that he was in then would likely continue until his death.

Those were the cold hard facts as she gave them. She never answered me when I asked why I had not been notified. No one had bothered to call me. It was not the first time that I felt the sting of medical judgment against the alcoholic. Bill and I were treated often to judgmental scrutiny by those who were in charge, and we felt their lack of compassion for the trap in which we found ourselves.

I tried to be quiet for a moment so that I could pray. Nothing had prepared me for this. This which I was looking at could not be real. The cruel words that the nurse had given me could not be real. It all seemed real enough, but it could not be the reality of the situation. God was real. If God were real, then this could not be real. My mind turned between the reality of God through His Son Jesus, and the reality of Bill's situation.

I made a call to Katherine. I could not call John as he was out of the country. I tried not to alarm her with this new turn in events. I couldn't answer her questions; I couldn't even answer my own. I kept telling myself to go back to the truth as I knew it; God is the reality in this situation! I had not known Him for very long but I knew without question that He existed, and I was putting all of my hopes in Him. I was determined to believe God and that He would heal Bill.

God's providence is often misunderstood by mankind, but I was calling on it with expectation. One of the heavy burdens that we bear at the end of alcoholism is the level of disdain with which the medical community views the alcoholic. Alcoholism usually has a very messy ending. It's costly and the patients usually have few personal resources left. It was no different for us. Our finances were down to nothing and while Bill was in the hospital there was no paycheck. However, I was learning about a greater truth, one unseen by the eye, but nevertheless more powerful than the natural world. I called upon God and

He opened new doors for us. He gave us better physicians, more wisdom and a new perspective.

I sat by Bill's bedside night and day. I sat one day, two days, three days, four - reading the Bible. I read aloud into this room which held the sounds of Bill's shouting. He yelled, I read. He twisted in fury, I read. He made growling sounds, I read. He jerked spasmodically, I read. I had been told that Bill's spirit could hear the Word of God. If I would strengthen Bill's spirit by filling it with the Word of God then the Spirit of God would overcome the spirit of this dreadful enemy who was trying to kill him.

I read aloud, sometimes softly, sometimes in tears. This was all that I knew to do and I was going to do it. Day in and day out, I read. Mostly from the Psalms, I read. The Bible that I was using had been given to me as a child. I had kept it with me throughout the years. I seldom opened it except on the occasion of the death of my parents, or of a close friend. It had never brought me any comfort before because I had not known the Author. Now it was my lifeline and with every word I read, I was pleading with God to save Bill's life. And He did!

That marvelous day, I remember it so well. Everyone thought that I was crazy, but on the 13th day of July, 1982, I knew that God would give us a miracle! Nothing had perceptively changed in Bill's condition, but in my heart I knew something had happened. The atmosphere was different, the oppression was lifted and even the room had changed. The doctors were still very pessimistic.

Medically, Bill didn't look any different, but I knew that something had happened.

Later that same day two women came to pray for him. I didn't know them personally, but they were part of a group that had been praying for us. They had been told about our situation and I was happy to meet them. They were strong women of faith. God had sent them to us. By now our son John had been called home, so they prayed for all of us.

That night things began to change. Physical things began to happen. Fear tried to enter my heart but the Lord stood with me and confronted the enemy. He gave our family its first great victory. The battle had been fierce and though I had been ignorant of spiritual things, I quickly learned that God was trustworthy. In the morning all the restraints were removed and for the first time in days, Bill lay quietly on his bed. By afternoon all the tubes were removed, a semblance of normalcy returned, and all was beginning to be right with my world.

Slowly but surely Bill recovered. By the end of the month he left that hospital and entered a drug rehabilitation program in a nearby city. After a thirty-day mandatory stay he returned home. He was now saved and sober, but tough times lay ahead.

During the following years we suffered. We struggled to put our marriage back together. It was no easy task, for we had sustained some heavy blows, some that even seemed mortal. The Lord was with us and we pushed on. Even though we were committed to the Lord and we were trying to follow in His ways life was difficult. Every day we faced new and painful experiences, every day new frustrations and fears.

God was not satisfied to rebuild our marriage on any part of the old. He tore down all that we had built up, our relationship with each other, our relationships with family and friends. God took them all in His hands and He changed them all. Painfully, brick by brick, He tore us down and just as painfully, brick by brick, He built us anew.

With each new revelation about Bill, my spirit would buckle and I felt that I could not go on. I had always trusted Bill, never having reason to doubt his love for me. God disclosed each reason and with great pain Bill confessed his sins, especially those which dealt with emotional infidelity. God continued to uncover evil in us wherever it might be found. He continued and we cried out with a new kind of pain. We were under the scrutiny of the Holy Spirit. He bolstered us, washed us, and led us through the mine fields, but He exploded every one.

I recalled a conversation, saying to the Lord, "I don't really need to know all this stuff. It would be easier for me to stay in ignorance, Lord." God is a tough master, He knew best. He peeled us like a fine chef peels onions, but we did all the crying.

When he was able, Bill returned to school. He sought a Masters Degree in Counseling. His return to the classroom was difficult for me. It was as if he were walking into the old trap again, but I knew that the Lord had engineered this plan. Bill's grades proved to us every day that God had done a great miracle. During those long weeks in the hospital with poisons in his blood pumping through his body, his mind had been protected by God. I recall vividly walking into his hospital room as he hid something under the covers. When I questioned him he sheepishly showed me a small scrap of paper. He was trying to write his name and could not. In time his mind was able to function as before. There was no permanent damage to his mind and the poisons had not been able to leave their mark on him. Bill's memory returned to him and he was once again able to study and recall what he had learned.

We lost Bill's mother during this time. On her deathbed she had prayed to receive Jesus into her heart so we knew that she was safe in God's loving arms. We were very fragile during this season of our life. It was supposed to be a time of healing but it didn't feel like it. Each new outrage against us was magnified and our nerves were raw as our lives were already difficult. "God is good," we kept saying. We repeated it through every experience. "God is good." That's what we held onto. Truthfully, once we knew Him, where else could we go?

Opening the ministry should have been our happiest day. That day, however, was clouded by the death of our last remaining family pet. She was a black Labrador named Molly and she was loved by all the family, especially Bill. Many of Bill's problems stemmed from the loss of a family pet during his childhood. Since that early occasion he had tried to keep his heart safe from being open to love, with all its ensuing pain.

Upon receiving his Masters Degree in Counseling, Bill resigned his position with the college and under God's leadership, we closed all the old doors. Together we walked to face the new one. God threw the door open wide and we walked through, filled with anticipation. We had owned a four-store commercial building for a number of years. It was in the heart of town. Tenant by tenant, the Lord had emptied the main part of the building of all commercial ventures. On August 18, 1985, we opened *"...in the Name of Jesus Ministries, Inc.,"* and we went into full time ministry. God had taken two old sinners, and by the work of His hand had prepared us for our life ahead. Though we had often called out for mercy, God knew what was ahead. Those steps which we would have eliminated because of the pain, He used to help us experience His ways, making us more able ministers to help others. When the last tenant left we were led to open "Luke 4:18 Christian Bookstore," to facilitate in the work and to help instruct the body of Christ.

Bob brought me back to the present with a gentle touch on my arm. For a moment I had forgotten where

I was. He said, "Are you ready to go to Aunt Gerry's? It's time to leave."

Dutifully, I followed them.

chapter 6

REMINISCING ABOUT AUNT GERRY

The LORD bringeth the counsel of the heathen to nought:
he maketh the devices of the people of none effect.
(Psalm 33:10)

We climbed the stairs to Gerry's apartment. Her companion nurse had been waiting for us. She let us in and took her seat next to Gerry. We were all pleased to see Gerry's condition and the improvement in her living situation. Weariness had settled into my spirit and I struggled with the moment. I tried to tell Gerry about Bill's death, but the words would not come. Only tears came. Bob quickly explained to her that Bill was gone. I glanced at her face and she at mine. We were both alive with pain. I, losing Bill, and Gerry, at 92, was tired of losing everyone. She had outlived so many that were close to her. She took my hand and slowly shook her head as the tears came. In typical Gerry fashion she brushed them away and became, once again, the hostess. She showed everyone around the apartment. Again my thoughts took flight.

In retrospect, it had been a little over a year since Gerry had come to live in Cocoa Beach. So much had happened to her. Our lives were touched by her situation and the only solution seemed to have her come and live with us.

We had been surprised one day with a call from the manager of Gerry's condominium in Palm Beach. She told us that Gerry's behavior had become unsettling to her friends and neighbors. Gerry and Bill's mother had lived for many years in a condominium in Palm Beach. They each had their own apartments in the same building. They had been there for each other, in times that were good and times that were difficult. Since the death of Bill's mother we had kept in touch with Gerry, but mostly by phone.

Bill took the three-hour trip south to survey the situation. He realized that something needed to be done. Gerry had no children of her own, so Bill put out a call to his brothers and to a cousin whom he barely knew. Finances were not a problem for Gerry, but it was clear that she could no longer live without some kind of care or supervision.

Her mail was in a messy heap, unopened and hidden away in secret places. Bill found important papers squirreled away in old empty candy boxes. Most of her mail was unanswered. Her eating habits had deteriorated to sugary treats and her place needed a good cleaning. Amazingly she was still driving her car, but that would soon come to an end. The insurance company was refusing to cover her any longer and Bill could see why. Her life was in such a mess that even Gerry was agreeable to changing her living status. All she asked was that we not put her in a nursing home.

After finding her records and glancing through them, Bill discovered that Gerry had sufficient income and could continue to live in relative independence, but her records were unbelievable. She never kept a checkbook balance and she never filled out any of the stubs. She used all of her checkbooks randomly and in no discernible order. She never numbered them or kept any kind of records at all. She seldom opened a statement when it came from the bank and finally, she just stopped paying her bills entirely. A temporary solution was reached when it was decided that Bill would look after her finances, pay her bills, and see to any other legalities. The cousin, whom I shall call Rachel, would fly down from New York on a regular basis and attend to housekeeping chores and help Gerry meet her social obligations. Bill knew that this was only a temporary solution. It would, however, buy us some well-needed time. Then we could ascertain the will of God for Gerry's life.

Months before all this trouble with Gerry had arisen, we had been making plans for a trip. God had promised our home church a trip to Israel. We had spent hours in preparation, poring over maps, making plans and looking forward to a marvelous time. Though Gerry's life was becoming our responsibility, we still felt that the Lord would have us make the trip.

The weekend before we left the country, Bill met with Rachel and Gerry. They knew his plans for Gerry's future. He had spoken with a lawyer and had set up an appointment for that very day. Bill had hoped to be able to accomplish some of his plans before we left the country. Rachel became reluctant, Gerry did not want trouble between them so Bill half-heartedly agreed to postpone the appointment with the attorney. He was not happy with the change in plans but nothing could be won by pushing. Bill called the lawyer, explained the situation and the meeting time was changed. They would meet when we returned from Israel.

Bill was bothered by his cousin's attitude. He had painstakingly shared all his plans and thoughts with her and his brother Bob. With their agreement he had worked with the lawyer by phone and everything was ready for Gerry's signatures. They had decided to establish a trust, write a will, and transfer Gerry's funds into an Estate Trust Account. Since Bill was the only family member who lived in Florida, he would then be named trustee. Rachel seemed agreeable to all these plans, but for the moment Bill could not budge her. The night before our departure she called and wished us a "Bon Voyage" We could never have doubted her affection nor foreseen her tragic end.

Israel was wonderful and once again I felt the kindred pull of my spirit to the land where God had written His Name. In this beautiful country He had given the world His Son and in doing so, He offered salvation to all mankind. It was a special trip and a special time and we relished the deep communion which we experienced with the Lord. The trip home was long and tiring. As we crossed our own threshold we felt the weariness settle into our very bones. All we really wanted was a few days at home to rest and recover from the hectic pace we had been keeping. We had jet lag, time lag, and body lag. We kept to our beds for the first day home as we were really too weary to function well.

Our rest, however, was interrupted by a telephone caller with a startling message. It was the manager of Aunt Gerry's condominium who gave Bill the unbelievable news of Rachel's death, by murder. Not ready to believe the report, Bill called her telephone number in New York City. He let the phone ring and ring but still there was no answer. He made a number of calls trying to trace the story and find the truth. Finally the operator was able to connect him with the proper officials. He spoke at last to the police detective who was in charge of the case. Bill explained who he was, his connection with Rachel, and he asked for any information concerning this terrible rumor. The detective told him that it was no rumor. It was the truth.

Rachel Morgana had been brutally beaten to death by her brother. He had then taped her hands together, covered her with plastic and put her in a plywood box which he had built after he killed her. He had done all of this in the same apartment where their mother, who was an Alzheimer's patient, lay. He then labeled the box "trash," and carried it, with Rachel inside, to a trash pickup site in the city not far from their apartment. He had then tried to get someone to stay with his mother so that he could make a quick trip to visit his aunt in Florida.

This incredible story unfolded. In our absence, in fact it was within days after our departure, Rachel had carefully followed Bill's plan for Aunt Gerry. She had, however, taken Gerry to a different lawyer, but the basic plan was followed. She had a will drawn up, naming her mother as the only heir. She then instructed the lawyer to set up a trust, naming herself as trustee. She had her legal residence changed using Aunt Gerry's address as her own, and though we did not learn it until much later, she had even transferred ownership of Gerry's car to her own name. After all of this she returned to New York with Gerry's will in hand to show her brother what she had accomplished. In an act of fury he had bludgeoned her to death in the apartment which they shared with their mother, Gerry's last remaining sister.

In life, Rachel had been an actress of some renown having been in many New York productions. She had also spent a number of years on the road touring with a well-known stage play. Television and newspapers boldly proclaimed this story of dark passions. Once her body was identified, they told and retold the story of Rachel's life and death. She had lived for years taking care of her mother, and apparently against good advice she had allowed her brother to move in with them. It was to be his temporary home until he could get some kind of job to support himself. Her brother had a long history of trouble. He was charged once with the shooting death of his own son. The boy broke into his father's home under the cover of night in order to steal some jewelry. There had been a trial. He was acquitted, and we, in Florida, lost touch with him.

Aunt Gerry was being plagued with queries from the local and New York papers. Television was playing and replaying this bizarre story so she found herself in the middle of a media frenzy. It created havoc in her relatively quiet life. Early one morning a strange woman with a child, stood at her front door. The woman loudly proclaimed that the child was the murderer's son. She wanted to know what Gerry was going to do about that. Gerry kept her wits and told the woman to leave her home. We knew that we had to move quickly.

We had labored getting her paperwork in order before our trip, so everything was pretty much up to date. It was obvious that we needed to protect her from the curious. We had no idea of the problems we might face but everything we did was covered with prayer.

The first annoying problem was the car. Arriving in Palm Beach, we realized that Rachel had driven Aunt Gerry's car to the airport, parking it there until her return. We did not know the car's license number so we could not identify the vehicle. We told the story to the airport security people. They were amazed by the twisted story and understood our dilemma, but without the license number they could give us no help. We needed to find the license number because without it we were unable to redeem the car. The car was just sitting there at the airport, costing money.

Meanwhile, Bill took Aunt Gerry to the lawyer whom he had originally chosen. Upon hearing the details of what had transpired, the lawyer was very cautious. He had been reading all about the story in the newspapers and he wanted to be absolutely positive about Gerry's competence. He recalled the earlier conversations with Bill and so he was aware of Bill's desires to protect Gerry. He asked Bill to leave the room so that there could be no undue influence as he spoke to Gerry about her desires. Rachel did not have time to transfer any of Gerry's money into the trust that she had set up, so the previous work became invalid. The new will was written based on some of the provisions from the old. The lawyer was patient and thorough and the work on Gerry's estate was finally completed.

While Bill was with Gerry at the lawyer's office, I had the happy task of trying to track down the license number of Gerry's car. I found no documentation anywhere in her apartment concerning her car. I placed calls to everyone I could think of. I called Gerry's insurance company, the tag agency, the police, everyone and anyone who might be able to help. I struck out everywhere.

Rachel had taken all the keys with her to New York... Gerry's apartment keys, car keys, and her mailbox keys. The mail box was filled to overflowing and I had no way to get into the box. We had explained our predicament to the postal officials, but the postman with the keys had finished his rounds for the day. There was no way to get in touch with him, so once again, we were stymied. Earlier in the week Bill had requested that the New York detectives send us Gerry's keys. They had no real need for them, but we surely did. They agreed to oblige us and send the keys by special delivery. While I was talking on the phone with someone at the tag agency again, there was a loud knock on the door. Hallelujah! It was the delivery boy with the keys. With a quick, "Thank you," I hung up the phone and accepted delivery of the package.

I went downstairs to empty the mailbox. It was a struggle to pull out the mail because the box was packed with three weeks' worth of mail. Rachel had taken the only set of keys, and Gerry had not been able to get into the box for her own mail.

Praise God! On the very top of the pile was a postal card from the Florida Department of Motor Vehicles. Gerry's payment was overdue for updating her automobile tag and this was her final notice. The tag number was clearly printed on the card. We finally had what we needed to retrieve her car.

The next day Bill and I went to the airport parking lot and claimed Gerry's car. We then met his brother and wife for breakfast. They had come down for a business trip, but they took time to meet with us as they wanted to hear about Gerry's situation before they went to visit her. We spent our breakfast time bringing them up to date on everything that we knew concerning Gerry, Rachel and the murder.

Our plans had been made. Bill was going to take Gerry's car back to her apartment and stay with her in Palm Beach, and I would take our car and go home to Cocoa Beach. My job was to try to locate a place for Gerry to live since she refused to live with us. She wanted her independence. We knew her driving days were over, so I needed to find her something close to us within easy walking distance to grocery stores, etc. As we left the dining room, having completed our "talking breakfast," Bob, Rosalie, and Bill walked me out to our car. It was parked next to Gerry's and as a joke, Bob asked, "Have you looked in the trunk?" Bill laughed and inserted the key and the trunk opened to reveal a surprise. We were surprised to find a new license plate hidden in the trunk with the new registration slip showing the car was now registered in Rachel's name, and a screw driver. Apparently she had not found the time to change the tags but she was well prepared to do so when she arrived back from New York. We stared with amazement and wonder. The Lord kept Gerry's car from being lost. If Rachel had been able to change the tag we would never have been able to properly identify the car. God had shown us once again that His protection covered us and covered those we prayed for. Every day seemed to open with new surprises and I wondered if this saga would ever end.

I drove back home and immediately went in search of an apartment for Gerry. We wanted her out of Palm Beach as quickly as we could manage it. I secured a place for her the next day. It was perfect. Bill made all the arrangements for the movers. He took her to the bank and had all of her accounts moved to the banks in our area. He took care of all the details of closing down her home. I laid the groundwork for opening her new one. Gerry had been forced to travel a tortuous and twisted path, but God had protected her. He had kept her safe until we could bring her to live near us. We were looking forward to the prospects of having Gerry become part of our daily lives.

Bill and I thought often about Rachel and her ultimate end. He had once spoken to her about the Lord. As she did with so many of the things Bill told her, she brushed it away with a quick remark, waving her hand as if to dismiss it. We joined in prayer for her before her death. Afterward, we could only pray that in that terrible moment before death, she had indeed called out to Jesus.

Once again, Bill's brother broke into my thoughts and brought me back to the present. He and his wife would now take me home. I needed to check the mail and pick up a few things, then I would drive Gerry's car back to Katherine's. They would stay in Cocoa Beach but we would be reunited tomorrow evening for dinner before the memorial service.

chapter 7

BILL'S MEMORIAL SERVICE

Son of man, behold, I take away from thee the desire of thine
eyes with a stroke: yet neither shalt thou mourn nor weep,
neither shall thy tears run down.
Forbear to cry, make no mourning for the dead,
bind the tire of thine head upon thee,
and put on thy shoes upon thy feet,
and cover not thy lips, and eat not the bread of men.
So I spake unto the people in the morning:
and at even my wife died;
and I did in the morning as I was commanded.
(Ezekiel 24:16-18)

 The day of great dread was upon me. It had been four days since Bill's death and now it was time for the public goodbyes. His memorial service was to begin at 7:00 in the evening. I seemed stuck somewhere between the actualities and the memories of life. I was stunned to realize that, though it felt like a lifetime, it had only been four days since his death. I was weary and lived in the midst of dread and resignation. I was determined to hold my emotions with a strong grip so that I might display my belief in God

and His sovereign ways. I had to project my faith in the eternal promise of God and come into agreement with His plan. In truth, however, I still fought a great inner turmoil against that which had happened.

I had not yet come into agreement with God. I was not even sure that the victory had been the Lord's. I wrestled each night with hearing the voice of Satan, proclaiming that the victory had been his. I knew that he was a liar, the father of lies, but his attacks were constant and merciless.

I pushed all these troubling thoughts away. I would deal with them later. I understood, with a wry smile, what Margaret Mitchell was saying through the character of Scarlet O'Hara. I would copy her and do what was set before me to do and think about my emotional state "tomorrow".

The family had made plans to gather at a restaurant near the ministry for a light meal before the service. Once again I was being driven back to Cocoa Beach. This time I was with Katherine and family, and even with Bill gone, I could reach out and touch him through them through the generations. They were, after all, flesh of his flesh and bone of his bone. It was a peculiar experience but a comforting one. They were so gentle with me even as they struggled to understand. If God loved them, then why did He take their grandfather from them?

It was John Palmer who first noticed the flags. We were in Cocoa Beach driving down A1A when he exclaimed,

"I guess Dave died, too." We looked with him as he pointed to the flag at a Wendy's restaurant. It was at half-mast. We noticed that other flags in town were at half-mast. I wondered who it could be that was so honored, and I felt a momentary empathy with the family of the deceased. I offered a short prayer, "Help them Lord, give them Your strength."

We parked in the ministry parking lot. I forced my feet to go inside, to carry me over the threshold. For so many years Bill and I had worked side by side in this building. I had not been here since his death. I was determined to be obedient to the Spirit of God. He had told me that many would be watching me tonight. Many who did not know Him were wondering and would be watching. Did she really trust God? Did she really know without a doubt that Bill was in heaven? These were some of the questions for which they sought their own answers. Their own mortality being shaken, they were being forced once again to look at death and their own final ends.

Taking a deep breath I went inside. What a transformation. Those of our home church, joined by a number of friends, had toiled faithfully. They had worked hard and they had changed a rather utilitarian complex into a wonderland of flowers and food. The auditorium had been arranged to accommodate the expected crowd. Extra chairs had been brought in and put in order. Large arrangements of flowers had been beautifully set about. Everything had been polished and cleaned. The guest book had been put in the reception area, and I noticed that people had already been there and signed their names. Bill's favorite picture of himself sat on the front desk in the reception area. In this picture he was holding a large freshly-caught sea trout. And the only thing larger than the fish was his smile. He seemed so alive in that picture, so happy, so content. I was glad to see him even if it was just in a picture.

Food had been beautifully prepared. Large tables had been set in buffet fashion in the room which we used to feed the hungry on Saturday nights. Everything was nicely arranged and appointed. Every detail had been attended to, there was nothing left undone.

The family had assembled at the restaurant. I had no hunger, but to keep peace, I toyed with some soup. We were all there. I sat in the midst of my family grateful that they were with me, but I was unable to reconcile the strong feelings of loss. One was missing. Bill was not there and that lack seemed greater than the remainder of the family. Would it always be this way, I wondered. Would the feelings of loss always overwhelm me and crowd out the future? Would I walk with this pain forever? Again, like Scarlet, I pushed these thoughts out of my mind. I prepared my heart to meet all those who would come to pay their respects and remember Bill.

The auditorium was beginning to fill with people. There were old friends that I had not seen in years, mixed in amongst those who were the newer friends of our Christian walk. There was a warm and comforting

Spirit present as the children and I were able to move with ease and take our seats.

Jimmy Smith and a mutual friend would conduct the service.

They were making their last minute preparations. They stepped down from the platform to greet me and to meet the family. People came to hug me, to offer a kiss on the cheek, a squeeze of the hand. There were gentle touches, given with love and compassion, which we gratefully received.

When the service began, I heard from heaven. God's voice, ringing in my spirit, spoke these words to me *"That which Bill accomplished since his conversion has been at My direction. He has been found faithful and obedient. You celebrate his life this evening, but I tell you, child, that which is before him is far greater than that which is completed. Have no fear, My daughter. That which he accomplished on earth holds him in good stead here. He stands with me now looking down upon the gathering and he is pleased. He loves you and he encourages you to continue without him. Be at peace, My daughter, for I am with you. You will find that My Grace is sufficient for you."*

It was an amazing experience. I could hear from God and listen to the service at the same time. I felt an excitement building in me and giving me strength. Amazingly, the dread was gone. I was able to relax and laugh as both men and reminisced and reminded us all of Bill.

He had been a man of compassion and humor. Frail, yes, but with a deep inner strength that comes from being obedient to God. He was the man whom I loved above all others.

Jimmy read from the prophet Isaiah, Chapter 58:6-12. He equated these words with the work that Bill had accomplished and declared that if Bill needed a name, he could be called the "repairer of the breach." That was my sweetheart they were talking about, and it was all true. Even God loved him. He loved him enough to take Bill home with Him.

They spoke to those who had known Bill, B.C.- that is before Christ had come into our lives. He laid the groundwork for each person in attendance to look to God for salvation, through Jesus Christ His Son. Both men testified that they represented just a few of the clergy that had been restored through this ministry.

Jimmy asked for those who had been spiritually touched by this ministry to raise their hands. It was awesome to see the number of hands. There were so many people. The children were deeply touched by the numbers. There were so many people who recognized their father's great gift for ministry.

Jimmy then sang some of Bill's favorite spiritual songs. He was always able to transport an audience into the presence of God with his magnificent singing voice. Music poured forth from him at the piano and in song. How rich it all was. These two men had interwoven their God-given talents and gifts to honor my beloved Bill. They had succeeded beyond his ability to request. They had poured out their hearts to God in celebration of Bill's life. I felt sure that, as they pleased God, they impacted everyone else in attendance.

The room was filled with a great mixture. There were old friends and new...the worldly and the spiritual...those with their spiritual eyes opened and some not as yet blessed... those who had received the promised deliverance and those who still lived on the other side of that great chasm.

I was amazed to see the seating which God had arranged. The chairman of the local A.C.L.U. sitting next to one of the county's most vocal advocates for the Right to Life; my cousin sitting with his present wife, and behind him was his ex-wife and her present husband, Aunt Gerry's companion tenderly holding her hands and giving encouragement. There were those who loved us but found our faith strange, sitting near those who stood with us in faith but really didn't know us very well. Friends of the children had come to stand with them. In the midst of this great occasion, God ministered to everyone and broken relationships were made whole. Jimmy was right, Bill was the repairer of the breach. Only God and Bill could get such a diverse crowd together. The old life and the new life joined together to say farewell to Bill.

The service was completed with more songs and then there were quick reunions with those who had come.

I was amazed at the size of the crowd. Many had been standing on the sidewalk, unable to even enter the building.

One young woman had walked barefooted, refusing rides when offered. She was honoring her pledge to Bill. He had asked her to no longer ply her trade and instead live for God. Because she was barefoot she would not come into the building but she did want to sign his book as an expression of her affection and gratitude for his ministry to her. It was a wellspring of love and affection. We in the family will always remember that night with fondness. That which I had dreaded, had by the grace of God, become a time for healing our all-too-broken hearts.

As we were leaving the now almost-deserted building, one of my good friends walked me out to the car. At the insistence of John Palmer, who had not forgotten about the flags at half-mast, I asked her who else had died. "Oh," she said, "That was for Bill. I called City Hall and told them that their pastor had died and they needed to honor him." We never bothered to verify her story because it pleased us. It was just like the Lord to give us something to smile about during the long drive back to Katherine's.

chapter 8

Home Alone

And she said unto them, Call me not Naomi, call me Mara:
for the Almighty hath dealt very bitterly with me.
I went out full and the LORD hath brought me home again
empty: why then call ye me Naomi,
seeing the LORD hath testified against me,
and the Almighty hath afflicted me?
(Ruth 1:20-21)

 A full week had passed since Bill's death and it was time for me to leave Katherine's. The safe harbor that I had found in the bosom of my family was a temporary one. There was work to be done at home and at the ministry. I still had obligations and I was now responsible for the upkeep of Aunt Gerry I felt a definite urgency to return home and face that which lay ahead. I don't think Katherine and John were as sure of my plans as I was, but I felt the stirring of the Lord moving me home. Into what circumstances, I did not know. I did know, however, that He was encouraging me to return to my home and to my work.

It was difficult walking into the house alone for the first time. We had lived in this house for over thirty years. I could not count the number of times that I had walked through the front door, but it had never been like this before. There was a real sense of the unreal. The first thing that I noticed was the silence. Everything was so quiet. Even the clocks had stopped. This was an eerie silence and it was an unaccustomed visitor in this home. I walked from room to room. Everything looked the same, but there was an absolute tomb-like quiet and it was unsettling.

The noise of life had always filled each room. Men, women, children, dogs, cats, snakes, birds, and other living things had all lived here at one time or another. They had all given of themselves to this place. Now there was nothing but silence. Where were the sounds of life, the laughter and tears? They had all made their mark, but now the walls kept their secrets well hidden from me. They stood mute. There was no longer any comfort here.

Just as Bill had been taken from me, so were the sounds of our life together. I was left with this dreadful quiet. This strange stillness that had settled over our home was slowly making its way into my heart.

The house seemed strangely larger and it was empty of all meaning for me. Cold and quiet on the inside, it was void of all purpose. Its purpose of giving safe harbor and comfort to the family was finished. Bill was dead and his house was dead too.

Though it was daytime, I switched on every light as I walked through each room. I turned on the radio and wound the clocks. I did everything that I could to break the hold that silence had forced upon our home.

I sat at Bill's desk to call the children. I had promised to call upon arriving home. I was determined to keep them from worrying about me. "I arrived safely," I said, "Aunt Gerry's car gave me absolutely no trouble." The car had become a family joke. It was the rusty old Chevrolet that Bill had begun driving since its rescue from the Palm Beach airport. The insurance company had finally refused to insure Aunt Gerry as a primary driver, so Bill and I had taken over the job of driving Gerry to any appointments she might have. Once Gerry's companion came into our lives, she used her van to transport Gerry. That left the "rust bucket" for Bill. Since receiving this car Bill and I had given our cars away, so this rusty old rattletrap was the only source of transportation I had. It wasn't much but I was grateful for it.

As I sat in Bill's chair at his desk, I looked around the room. We built this house while John was still in a crib and this had been his baby room. It had become his little boy's room and remained his room all through his high school days. After he left home it served as an extra room until it finally became Bill's den.

I sat there looking at the room, trying to understand exactly what had happened to us. The room had not changed. Bill's mementos, pictures and keepsakes were still all displayed. Some things had real value, but mostly the value was only sentimental. I turned in Bill's large swivel chair and looked at the wall behind me, crowded with memorabilia. Mounted fish, their bodies arched in flight, were fixed in time and space next to his four framed college degrees. There were also plaques bestowed upon him by learned men. The degrees and plaques seemed to shout at each other, proclaiming their own importance, as if they could best tell the story of Bill's life. All of these things were Bill's and they were once important to him.

This room was filled with the mark of his life, but it gave me little comfort. He was gone and this room reflected him in life but death had gotten a hold on him. Death had wrestled with me for him and won. Death had won and I was left with this room. Futility filled me, and with a shuddering sob I lay my head on his desk and wept.

The pain came from so deep within that I thought I might break. I had wanted to be alone so that I might be free to express my emotions. I was no longer forced to hold myself in for others. Now for the very first time since Bill's death I was alone and able to really let go. The grief came in waves, breaking over me and for a moment I was fearful of drowning. My heart felt as if it were pressed against my throat and if I would let it, it could come right out of my mouth, with my sobs. Tears wet my face as I looked around the room again. With a shake of my head I shouted, "These things are not the evidence of Bill's life. These are temporal things and they have no real value." I touched his pictures, the computer where he had spent so much of his time. I touched his books stacked at the end of his massive desk. As I went out the door I touched his fishing hat and said another goodbye. I would say goodbye many times again but none would be more poignant.

I walked through the house again and saw clearly that nothing in our house had any worth. Bill's life had merit, but now he was gone. He was gone and that which he left was worthless. Without him, the purpose for his home had been accomplished. There was monetary value, yes, but with an eye on eternity, everything here became valueless to me. These things, however beautiful, were not the measure of his life. They did not speak the truth of our many years together.

A long time ago Bill and I had read a book entitled *On Death and Dying*. It was written by Elizabeth Kubler-Ross and was published in the late 1960's. It was a book for those who were facing terminal illness. It was for them and their loved ones. She had carefully isolated the five separate stages of grieving and dying. I thought about that book now, trying to recall all that she had said, hoping to find a clue for me.

Stage one - was about denial and isolation

Stage two - spoke of anger

Stage three - told of bargaining

Stage four - was depression

Stage five - was final acceptance

I wondered where I was on that graph, or if I was off the chart entirely. I promised to find that little book someday, but at the moment there were other things to attend to.

Bill's desk needed to be changed. Once again led by the Spirit, I was in his den. I heard the Lord say, "Prepare Bill's desk to your way." I finally understood. Bill had been left-handed and I was right-handed. So that I might fully understand each situation and be able to respond to Aunt Gerry's needs, I needed to rearrange Bill's desk. I spent the rest of the day getting files, drawers and papers in an order that I could more easily comprehend. I could not understand the urgency, but I was obedient to the nudging of the Holy Spirit, and it felt pretty good to keep busy.

I felt that it was important to show Gerry that though Bill was gone, stability would prevail in her life. I would continue as Bill had, managing her affairs, paying her bills and seeing to her needs. With this in mind I drove over to see Gerry.

As I drove to her apartment I thought again about the events that led to her moving closer to us. Since the death of Bill's mother we had not spent much time with Gerry. Bill used to call her regularly to find out how she was. She was an accomplished liar and always told us that she was just fine. We were certainly not prepared to see the deterioration of her life. We had always loved her and she was well-bonded to the family, especially to her nieces and nephews, their children and grandchildren. Everybody loved Gerry and it was not a hardship taking her as our responsibility. We felt much like rescuers bringing her here to live near us. She would not accept our invitation to live in our home but she was willing to come and be near us.

I found a nice, though small, apartment just a few blocks from our home. She would be very well situated, a short walk to the grocery store, pharmacy and a variety store. She could get her hair cut or satisfy a need for Crystal burgers. Gerry had always been a person who enjoyed a walk so this place seemed ideal. For the first few days after she moved in everything was good. It didn't take long, however, to realize that she would need a companion housekeeper. The Lord brought us a very special woman.

She came to us through an agency but in truth she was a gift from God. She needed a home and we needed a caregiver. She was a Christian nurse, and though Gerry did not instantly become a happy camper, she finally understood. She resigned herself to the fact that this woman was to be a part of her life. There were moments of real rebellion, but Gerry finally settled into this new phase of her life. She was ninety-two years old and accustomed to doing pretty much as she pleased. There were some real adjustments made by both of these women as they struggled in their new relationships—their relationship with us and with each other.

I will never forget the evening her companion called to tell us that Gerry had lost her teeth. Gerry hated wearing them and would often hide them. It soon became apparent that her teeth were destined to become their funniest quarrel. It seemed that Gerry, in a fit of temper, had pitched them out of the car window. She kept her secret until confronted by her companion, but it was too late to do anything about it. They had gone too many miles down that road. Gerry had made her point and no one ever mentioned her teeth again. Bill and I had been grateful to God for Gerry's companion and for the marked improvement that we saw in her. With Bill gone I found that I called upon her even more and I was very appreciative for her help.

Bill's desk, large and sturdy, became my work place. He had been a creature of habits. Upon rearranging all the files, I found everything in perfect order. One by one, I completed the assignments on the funeral director's list. They had given me a long list of the necessary steps that I must take, to walk back from the edge of death. I had immediately notified the Social Security office to stop Bill's checks. I had made application for the widow's survivor benefits. Our attorney had graciously taken on the responsibility for notifying Bill's life insurance companies.

I started a new file and it was marked, "Bill's Final Papers." At first it only held his death certificate and a copy of his autopsy. The autopsy answered those often-asked questions about Bill's liver. He died of hepatic failure due to acute cirrhosis of the liver. God had kept Bill alive since that dreadful time when his liver had solidified. He lived a full and wonderful life with a diseased liver. God had not given Bill a new liver, He had made the damaged one function. Bill had lived successfully in this condition for nine years, to the day. The date of his death was, July 13, 1991. It had been on July 13, 1982 when I had received the revelation that he would be healed.

My financial situation was bleak at best. It seemed impossible to believe that I could survive. Only as God moved on the hearts of men could my situation change. I understood all too clearly that God had me in a place of miracles. In the natural there was no hope. In Bill's wallet at the time of his death was a five dollar bill. On his desk was a box which held rolled and unrolled pennies. The pennies came to the princely sum of thirty-eight dollars. The small bank books, which once registered the grand totals of our savings accounts, now held only a history, a history of giving not saving. Money once so carefully saved was gone. Our savings accounts had long since been drained for the work of the ministry. Aside from the few hundred dollars that were in our checking account, I was broke. Bill was gone, our money was gone, everything was gone!

Bill and his money had run out at the same time. Amazingly enough I had no real fear. I had become numb to natural events. I could only trust God. We had poured everything we had, or were, into the ministry. God called us to help those who could not as yet help themselves. We had spent our time, our strength, and all of our resources on behalf of those less fortunate. We had put all of our hope and trust in the God of all creation to meet our needs. We had given all that we had, but in the long run we considered it a very good investment. We had been obedient to the Scripture that had been read at Bill's memorial service. The scripture reads as follows: *"Is not this the fast that I have chosen? to loose the bands of wickedness, to undo the heavy burdens, and to let the oppressed go free, and that ye break every yoke? Is it not to deal thy bread to the hungry, and that thou bring the poor that our cast out to thy house? when thou seest the naked, that thou cover him; and that thou hide not thyself from thine own flesh?" (Isaiah 58:6-7).*

Every day a miracle came forth. People gave gifts to the ministry in Bill's memory, and some gave gifts to me for my personal use. As I trusted God, He brought forth the finances to pay each bill. Even the hospital and the undertaker received full payment in just a few months. I moved through those first few weeks in obedience to God. He gave me the strength and the will. I had no will of my own to live. I wanted to be with Bill, not here in this terrible world. God's power made me walk on. It was certainly not by my will, but by His. I could call on God with all assurance of His answer because Bill had been faithful to tithe and to give gifts and offerings. In the natural realm it looked bad but in the supernatural realm I was in very good shape because Bill had given all that he had. As widows we need to continue the practice of tithing. We should not expect to receive from God if we have not been obedient to His Word.

During this time, if things could break, they did. If things could fail, they did, and if things could shake, they did. At the ministry one of the freezers failed, and it was loaded with food for the hungry. Toilets seemed balky and were often tempted to an overabundance. A drunken sailor broke the glass door leading to the bookstore. He had mistakenly thought it was the entrance to one of the many topless places in the area. Everything was a battle. Sometimes the battle was just my will against the plan of God. Though I was determined to be obedient to God, every day there was a new and difficult confrontation. I was experiencing the difficulties one encounters marking the passage into widowhood. I was forced to go into a place where I did not want to go and sip from a cup which I did not want to drink. I was forced to walk down a path I did not choose.

I asked Him, again and again, why He had given me a scripture to believe that Bill would once again be healed. Why had He done that, if all the time God had intended to take Bill home? It was an ever-burning question inside of me. When I would ask Him, He would turn me to the scriptures which told the story of Jesus in the Garden of Gethsemane. He, too, had been forced by obedience to take a cup which He did not want and to walk a path not of His choosing. I came to realize that without His obedience I could not be obedient, and without His servanthood, I could not serve. He had accomplished it first, and it had been done for me and those like me.

All of us who call ourselves the children of God are called to die. None of us can escape our destiny which is a slow climb to the cross, His cross. The cross of Jesus becomes our own, when we are called to die. I am not speaking of the natural death but the death of self, the death of our hopes, plans, dreams and ambitions. Our soulish parts need to perish and as our fingers grip His cross, we can let death happen. When we glory in Him and accept that which He would do for us, then we can let go of all our personal desires. The secret is to come into agreement with God's plan, even when we hate it. We will find that it is often a way filled with pain and sorrow as we die to flesh, but if we will yield to Him in obedience we can then be called the Sons of God and our lives will be fruitful and fulfilling.

My first Sunday back at the Tab was a blessing. Though I was very tired and my heart was still raw and broken, I hungered to be with the body of Christ. I took my accustomed seat and memories flooded me. I looked up and saw Jamie approaching. He had been fighting his own fight with death, but God was still mightily using him in ministry. He took my hand and gently asked, "Can you take correction from your pastor?" I smiled and nodded my head in agreement. "You told me that Bill should have died nine years ago but that God had given him nine extra years of life." Again I nodded in agreement. "No honey" he said, "I was praying for you yesterday and thanking the Lord for extending Bill's life by nine years. God told me that He had not given those years to Bill. He had given them to you. To Bill He had given eternity."

My hand flew to my heart. "Oh, Jamie" I cried, "That fits, it just fits the hole in my heart." Once again a word from the Lord would bring healing. Every day I was given a new revelation, every day a fresh touch.

Though I often felt that my pain was too great to heal, faithfully through the unction of the Holy Spirit, God would touch me and calm the storms within.

It was not many months after this conversation that Jamie, too, went on to be with the Lord. I know his family misses him and walks in their own pain and travail. Also his church misses him — his personality was deeply stamped on the Tab. The Christian world misses him. There are many great men in the body of Christ, but there was only one Jamie.

chapter 9

LOSING AUNT GERRY

All this is come upon us; yet have we not forgotten thee,
neither have we dealt falsely in thy covenant.
Our heart is not turned back,
neither have our steps declined from thy way;
Though thou hast sore broken us in the place of dragons,
and covered us with the shadow of death.
(Psalm 44:17-19)

It was now the second Saturday since Bill's death. I was sitting at his desk writing letters and was startled by the telephone when it rang. It was Gerry's companion. There was an urgency in her voice. "I've called for the ambulance. Gerry is having trouble breathing," she said.

"I'll dress and meet you at the hospital," I responded. I made a quick call to someone in our home church for prayer, dressed and headed to the hospital. "Not again, Lord," I pleaded in prayer, "Please, not again".

I moved Gerry's car into the Saturday traffic. It was a beautiful summer morning and cars were filled with happy people on their way to the beach. Surfboards, beach umbrellas, coolers, hampers and laughing people, all headed to sun and fun. Again, the joy of life was headed in one direction, but I was forced to travel in the opposite direction.

Gerry was 92. Bill's death had taken its toll on her usual spark for life. We had noticed that she had become quiet of spirit. She was definitely not her old self. She had outlived so many, but she had borne her sorrows well. Bill's death, however, seemed to drain her of her own life flow. I didn't know exactly what was wrong, but she certainly was changed. I prayed that her mourning would soon pass and that she would once again become the Gerry that we all knew and loved.

I pulled into the parking area nearest the emergency room entrance. She was at the nurses' station, and I went to stand beside her. I offered to help, but she seemed to have everything well in hand. She gave them Gerry's Medicare and hospitalization insurance numbers and answered all the nurse's questions. My heart once again said, "Thanks Lord, thank you for this woman!" I knew that in my condition I would not be able to handle any of this right now.

The room was active with people. Some of them recognized me and they nodded their heads in acknowledgment. It was as if none of us could believe that I was back in this place again and so soon. Gerry's companion completed all the forms and we walked into the waiting room. We were soon joined by others who had come to pray and stand with us in faith for Gerry's life. I felt like I was not only caught up in a bad movie, but I was being forced to sit through it, a second time.

I asked if Gerry had been baptized. "No, not yet, we were going to do it next week."

I looked at her, shook my head, and answered, "I don't think we will have a next week."

They had not been worshiping with us at our church, but had selected one a little nearer to home. Gerry had experienced conversion when she prayed with Bill to accept Jesus in her heart. She had received the peace of the Lord as it settled over her. She became content to go with her companion, wherever that might be. That church had accepted Gerry and they were prepared to give her a water baptism.

Suddenly Gerry's companion left the room to return a few moments later. She was carrying a small basin of fresh water, and she said "Follow me". I trailed behind her. To my horror, I noticed that she was headed directly for Emergency Room Number 1.

Every part of my mind shouted, "NO! I CANNOT GO IN THERE AGAIN! Oh God, I can't do it, I just can't! My emotions overwhelmed me. Hot tears streamed down my face. She boldly opened the door, walked through, and I obediently followed. Gerry lay on the same cold table which just two weeks before had claimed Bill. Nurses were bending over her, working to clear her lungs. That which had begun as a cold had quickly turned into pneumonia. They looked up from their work surprised to see us. Her companion announced, "The niece has come to baptize her."

My body went through the motions but my mind was in retreat. I didn't want to be here. My pain was still too fresh. I hated this place. It had sucked the very life out of Bill and now Gerry was its captive. What could I do? My mind was screaming at God, but I calmly baptized Gerry. I poured the fresh water on her and I bathed her in my tears. She was not conscious of my ministrations but I could hear her heavy breathing. After I made the sign of the cross on her forehead we turned and left the room.

As I exited Emergency Room Number 1, I cried out, "Lord, I don't do this kind of work."

His response was quick. "You will do anything I put your hands to." I nodded in agreement with Him and went to pray with the others.

Gerry lived just a few more days. They moved her to the intensive care area and she never left that area alive. Gerry's life, itself a book, had been rich and full. Those of us who knew her were blessed by that knowing. Her church promised to hold a small memorial service for her after the regular Sunday Service the following week. Once again our family would be called together, meeting to release its dead. Though they in the church had not known her very long, only sharing in the last few months of her colorful life, they honored her. The family who loved her was grateful.

Once again I was returning to an empty house, alone. I was afraid to imagine what else could happen. I didn't want to think about the possibilities, but I knew that anything was possible. I threw myself across the bed and cried. I couldn't help wondering if my family would be taken from me, one member at a time, until there were no more. I thought about all those difficult years of ministry. Did they not count for something in God's eyes?

Thus I reflected on my loss column. God had stripped away so much from us. It had been only three months after going into full time ministry that our store had been vandalized and destroyed by fire. The fire investigators said it was arson. Unknown men, covering up their evil deeds, had broken into the back of our store. They had stolen the $3.84 in coins which had been left in the cash register, and then they had set the place ablaze. It was a terrible mess. Clothing, bathing suits and lingerie, all terribly burned. Everything needed to be identified, itemized, and inventoried.

The office was in the worst condition since that was where the fire had been started. The business history of the store was destroyed. Files, records, orders, and sales slips were left as so much sooty garbage. The things that were being held on layaway were unrecognizable. We had to sit together, the clerks and I, and try to remember all the garments that had been set aside. We had to try and remember who bought the items and how much money had been put down. It was a grueling task, dirty and discouraging. Who had done this awful thing to us, and why? We had hurt no one. All we wanted to do was to be of help to mankind. We trudged through the cleanup in a state of wondering.

We could not believe the attitude of the insurance adjuster. Bill's family had sold insurance for years but this kind of an attitude was new to us. They questioned and accused. It was not bad enough that we had lost so much in the store, now they would take our reputation. Our agent was wonderful, and after we complained to him the adjuster and his crew left us in peace.

We were new in ministry and had not yet realized the full extent of the cost to serve the Lord. We had very little - alcoholism and the ministry had taken the lion's share, and now God was demanding that small portion which remained. He was demanding the last of what we had, as if He would let nothing stand between us and Him. Even though we had willingly given the store over to Him, His plan took us by surprise.

I asked Him once why serving Him was so reminiscent of an old movie scenario. We have all seen those old pictures when the fat lady is about to sit down and someone would pull the chair out from under her. She would fall, roll on the floor, and the audience would grab their sides with laughter. He responded, "It's a great deal like that".

I quickly retorted, "Lord, that's just not nice!"

"Yes," agreed the Lord. "But child, how else will you learn that when the chair is pulled out from under you, I will be faithful to catch you?"

He was right of course. There was no other way. We would not trust God with just His Word. We had all been given plenty of opportunities to show Him that we would trust Him, but we seldom did. In times of calamity we would turn to Him, because we usually had nowhere else to turn. God was right. Hard as it all was, He had been right. It was in the trials and the testings that we would come to know Him and His faithfulness. The fire had cost us well over $100,000.00. We were grossly underinsured and so we suffered an immense financial loss.

From the beginning, "...*in the Name of Jesus Ministries, Inc.*", had been a raging battle. We had opened with such joy, imagining all the wonderful things that the Lord would do. A few months later we were in a struggle just to survive. It seemed that there were those who did not want us in the city and they did their level best to close the ministry down. The local zoning ordinances did not allow for a church to be at our location. Ironically, I was serving at the time as vice-chairman of the City Planning Board. In a surprise letter, the city gave us exactly 72 hours to cease being a religious organization. The violation had come to the attention of the city through an anonymous telephone caller!

Our attorney promptly contacted the City Building Department, as they had lodged the complaint. No matter what she said or did, they were adamant. According to them we had violated the zoning ordinance, so we must close. We continued to minister. We were just as determined as they were. Every day we went to the Lord with this pressing matter, all God would say was, "PERSEVERE".

Finally we were subpoenaed by the Code Enforcement Board. They notified us of a public hearing and the date was announced. In the body of the subpoena, the list of fines and penalties that could be levied against us was printed. If everything in the subpoena was correct, and we were adjudicated to be guilty, then we could be fined up to $250.00 for each day that we had been in violation. The struggle had lasted for many months and could have rendered us totally insolvent.

In all the days, weeks and months that we had been harassed by the city, no guardian of civil authority had ever visited us. The property had never been inspected and our accuser had not, as yet, been identified by the city. No representative of the city had ever crossed our threshold, but they still would not yield. They were determined to close the ministry down. The last conversation we had at city hall ended with a shouting match. No man was ever more determined to close a place down. With all the other possible selections in Cocoa Beach, we the Christians were identified as the undesirable ones.

We were sure that this ministry, in the center of town, was the will of God. We fasted, we prayed, and we held our ground. Just two days before the public hearing, a man representing the city finally came to inspect the ministry. This was the same man who had declared that he would shut us down. Bill escorted him into his office, and I guess Bill startled him when he bent his head to pray. Bill asked God to bring forth the truth, to illumine for this man all that was right with the work which we were doing. He asked God to disclose any violations at the ministry or to disclose any intent to defraud the city. When Bill was finished praying the man looked stunned. Bill said it was as if he had never heard prayer before. The man seemed changed. Bill walked him through the complex and uncovered everything that had been in question. God had given us His word, that this was "a piece of cake" for Him, and He told us not to fear. It's difficult not to fear when all hopes and dreams have been threatened, but we were determined to be obedient to God. Fearfully, we did not fear.

When the inspection was concluded this man, who had been determined to close the ministry, found nothing wrong. Not in the building, the parking lot, nor in the work which we were doing. Now it was time for Bill to be stunned. The man even volunteered to speak on our behalf to the Code Enforcement Board. He promised to assure them that there was no cause for alarm and that everything was in compliance with the city. The battle was won! God had said that it would be a piece of cake, and indeed it was.

The work we were doing had its own difficulties. Strife and competition from others caused us much heartache. We became determined to speak no ill of any other ministry or church. The more they accused us, the more we bent in prayer. We did what the Word of God told us to do, but I cannot say that it was easy.

We were not a church, so we could not rely on regular weekly offerings. Aside from a few loyal and generous souls, the finances came from us. Once we had been people of means, but we had given all that we had into the work of the Lord. Very few people knew that the money to keep the ministry afloat came from our own pockets. We had spent our retirement income, our investment capital, and everything that we had saved for our old age. As it stood right now, with Bill gone and his life insurance in question, I could neither retire, become ill, nor grow old.

I lay in bed with these scenes playing across my mind. The phone interrupted my thoughts. It was my good friend Essie Sprow. She was summering in North Carolina and called to encourage me. She invited me to come up for a visit. Nothing could please me more. I wondered at her timing. Had she called yesterday, I could not have left Gerry. I wondered about Gerry's car, if it would make such a trip. I told her that I would try to make some arrangements and promised to return her call. It was reassuring to hear her voice. She never changed, she was always there when she was needed, always willing to give comfort and love. I wanted to go and be with her, to throw myself on her mercy, but I was hesitant about my transportation.

Again the phone interrupted my thoughts. This time it was Katherine. Her husband was going to make a business trip to North Carolina and she and the children had decided to join him, extending the trip into a holiday. Would I like to come along? Katherine also suggested that if I wanted, maybe I could visit my friend Essie. They could drop me off there.

How good God is! Once again the Lord was making a way for me. It took just a few days to prepare and we were on our way. God had not only provided a destination but a joyous way to travel. Time to spend with my family and my dearest friend; they would minister to me as few others could. And God would let me drink in the beauty of His mountains which I loved so much. What a blessing!

chapter 10

SELLING AND MOVING

The LORD will destroy the house of the proud:
but he will establish the border of the widow.
(Proverbs 15:25)

 The impromptu family trip was wonderful, but I was coming home to emptiness again, and it was hard. I now felt particularly ill-suited to our home. It was no longer ours. With the loss of Bill, it had been stripped of all that was important to me and left just a shell. The life was gone. I had lived in this place for over thirty years, but now I found it devoid of all life. Even the memories were somehow gone. This was no longer Bill's home, and it soon became apparent that it was no longer mine.

The Lord reminded me that two years ago, we entertained a young family for a Christmas meal. We had come to know the Rizzo family through the ministry. We had admired and respected them, and it was easy to love them and their children. After dinner, as Lorraine and I worked together in the kitchen, I heard the voice of the Lord. "This is to be her kitchen," He said.

"May I tell her Lord?" I asked.

"No, not yet. The time is not right," He responded.

I kept the secret in my heart until Bill and I were alone that night. I relayed to him that which I had heard, and he quickly agreed. "That's the Lord," he said. We were not really surprised since we felt that there were changes coming for us. Bill had hoped that it would mean a time of rest and leisure. We were both eager to move on in the things of the Lord and being called to give up our home to this family posed no problem for us. In fact, in our minds and spirits, the deed was already done. We felt that the day would come when we would move on and they would move in. We were glad that once again this house would be filled with an active family. But who could have guessed that Bill would go first, leaving me far behind. Bill was now free, but I was still under the constraints of this world.

I called Hollie, our home church pastor, to tell her of my return from North Carolina. She was the only person in whom we had confided concerning the Rizzos having our home. During our conversation she told me that she had heard that the couple had found a house in a nearby area. Another good friend who was in the real estate business, was looking for a house for them. They were definitely in the market for a home.

They were in a difficult position. Their lease was up but the owner would not renew. He was making plans to return to that location himself so they had to find a place quickly. The Lord had told them to pack, but they had found no suitable place to rent or buy. In obedience they had packed and were struggling with the problems of house hunting while living out of boxes.

I had wanted to say something to them before I left for North Carolina, but the Lord kept me mute. Now upon hearing that they were considering a house which they had found, I questioned again whether I heard the voice of God. My confidence had been badly shaken during the last few weeks.

When I hung up the phone, I prayed. I asked, "Should I call her now Lord?"

"No," He said, "I have taken care of everything."

"Yes, Lord," I said, "Please Lord, your will be done. Lead me Lord and tell me what to do. I am not able. I will rely on you."

Suddenly the phone rang. It was Lorraine. She was checking to see if I had returned. "I hear you've found a house." I said.

"No," she responded. "Jimmy liked the house because it had a pool, but when we prayed, we knew that it was not for us."

"Now, Lord?" I asked in silent prayer.

"Now," He said. "You may tell her now."

"Honey," I asked, "How would you and your family like my house?"

"Oh no," she cried, "We can't afford it."

"Don't be too sure," I said, and then I told her the words that the Lord had given me that Christmas evening, over two years ago.

God will confound the wisdom of the wise. The rules, that for generations have set the standards for widows, were certainly broken and re-broken in my situation. Conventional wisdom decrees that a widow should make no major changes for at least a year. What magic men can find in a year is beyond me. Though selling my house within six weeks after Bill's death did fly in the face of rational thinking, I had absolute peace about God's plan. I thought back, remembering with amazement that God had allowed me to talk to Bill about this plan. We had prayed together about this word, and we had come into agreement that this was to be their home. God was making a huge and sudden change in my life, but He didn't put me in the position of plowing this new field alone. He had let me consult with Bill about this plan and we had agreed together with God. We knew that this was indeed His plan.

I had no hesitation about this family having our home. In fact, it would be wonderful for them to have this house. It would also be wonderful for the house to have this family. As yet I didn't know what I was going to do or where I would move, but I was well-pleased with the plans that the Lord had made to bless this dear family.

My attempts to reach my friend in real estate were met with disappointment. I was told that she was out of town and could not be reached. I went down to the Ministry to tell my secretary that I was back. It was my surprise to see her talking with my realtor. These two women were becoming acquainted and I didn't have a clue as to how important these two young women would become in my life.

Lojuan had come to the ministry under difficult circumstances. Before she had moved, Bill's secretary had spent the day with her, showing her the basic routine. The teaching would be done by the Holy Spirit, as He responded to each situation. He would train her, and with each experience she would become adept. She had big shoes to fill, but I knew that God had directed the choice. Once again the Lord had given us His grace, in that during Bill's last hospital stay he and I had been able to pray together concerning Lojuan's selection.

The girls responded eagerly as I told them about the Rizzos buying our home. To Carolyn I said, "You pray and hear the Lord about all the legal and financial particulars, because my mind is numb and I just can't think about business arrangements right now."

Agreement, that's what we had. Total agreement and everyone was thrilled at what the Lord was doing. It was very exciting. Since I was well aware that this was the will of God, I also could join in their excitement. Watching the unfolding of the will of God is a thrilling experience. Even though I was besieged by loss, I was able to rejoice with the Rizzos as they came to inspect their promised new home.

The Rizzos had been faithful to God. They, too, had struggled with loss but God was blessing them. He had given them His salvation, His Spirit, and His love. Now He was giving them something even more tangible. The children ran down the hall, just as my children had done. They skipped into each room as their parents made the bedroom assignments. The rooms were all inspected, and we laughed and cried together.

When I mentioned that I had a washing machine but no dryer, Lorraine laughed and said, "That's OK, I have a dryer but no washing machine." Everything fit together perfectly, in His timing and in His way.

They took an opportunity to take my hands and pray. We were standing at the foot of Bill's roomy chair when Jim lifted his voice to God. He was fervent in his thanksgiving prayer. My eyes filled with tears but everything was absolutely right. This was indeed the family God had chosen to live in our home. I knew that Bill was pleased, God was pleased, and I was pleased. No matter the circumstances or the turmoil, when you come into agreement with God, there is peace.

The Lord had shown me that I was to move into Aunt Gerry's condominium. At the time of purchase, Bill and

I had been added to the deed, to satisfy those who were uneasy about Gerry's age. They felt that at 92 Gerry was too old to be buying a condominium. They took this means of protection against the possibility of one day being forced to deal with her estate. By taking this step, the apartment was never included in Gerry's estate. With death striking twice, I ended up as the sole owner of this condominium. God had provided once again and I had a home to move into. Amazingly enough it all happened within four months after Aunt Gerry closed on this property. Again I saw the clear provision of the Lord.

Everything moved so quickly after the major decisions had been made. Gerry's companion stayed on at the condo for a few days until she could make other arrangements. I moved into Gerry's condo on Labor Day. In the six weeks since Bill's death, I had said goodbye to him, to Aunt Gerry, sold my home, stored my furniture, and moved into her small, unfamiliar apartment. Everything had happened so quickly my mind had really not been able to comprehend it all. I found myself surrounded by the remnants of another's life, while my own had been safely stored away. I didn't know what was ahead for me and I really didn't care. My foundations had slipped away from under me and I lived in a quiet despair.

Those who moved into my home helped me move out of it. Since, in obedience to God they were packed and ready to move, they were able to help me. And the young people of our home church, along with my children, helped me move. My belongings and furniture would go into storage. I would take very little to Aunt Gerry's. Our bed and a few small things were all I would need. I felt that the Lord was separating me from all my earthly possessions. I was coming into unknown territory, and I really did not need any reminders of what my life had once been.

Separation is never easy. I had become so hollow and empty inside, that there was plenty of room for the pain associated with breaking up my home and sadly, doing it alone. I worked a little at a time in each room of our house. Family pictures would come down. They would be wrapped for storage. Walls became bare and lonely. Drawers were emptied, Bill's clothing was given away. My mother's china was wrapped and carefully packed away. Clocks were dismantled, closets were emptied, and packing boxes soon littered each room.

As I gave up my home, I gave up Bill. I offered him up to the Lord. Each day I gave more of him away to God. I packed his belongings and gave him up. I let go of him, one box at a time, closing the lid on our life together.

At night, I would wander through the house which was no longer mine. I tried to remember better times, but reminiscing seemed to need a partner and I had none. One night I fell against the hall wall and wept. How could God expect me to do this? How could I go on? I cried out to the Lord. "I can't do this! How can I, Lord?"

God's voice strengthened me as He answered: "My child, I have taught you to live one day at a time. That is how you will live."

I thought to myself, I can do that. I can live one day at a time and God will see me through each day.

Moving into Gerry's was its own real adventure. There had been no time to freshen the apartment, and Gerry's furniture was old and needed attention. I know my friends didn't understand why I chose to live with her belongings instead of my own fine pieces. I don't think anybody really understood why I put my life totally behind me. I chose, instead, to live with her rather old and shabby furniture. I felt like it fitted me, for I too had become old and shabby. I felt that it was important for me to shut out my life as it had been and seek that which God had arranged for me.

John and Katherine came to help me move. I know that the move was no easier for my children than it was for me. I was grateful that God had put it in their hearts that I needed to move, and not be pressured to stay in the house where they had been raised. We all did our jobs, working carefully, but trying not to think about what we were doing.

Not since I had been a student in boarding school had I lived in communal housing. I was totally unprepared for the lack of privacy. It took me some time not to expect Bill with the sound of every closing car door. I would often jump with expectation when I heard a car in the parking lot. Gerry's personal things were still in her apartment. There were papers, pictures, and mementos. I forwarded them to the correct parties, but I felt as if I was stuck in death and would be dealing with its aftermath for the rest of my life.

I just kept living, one day at a time. My schedule at the ministry kept me busy counseling, and my time in Gerry's apartment kept me seeking the Lord. The days were tough but the nights were tougher. My emotions ranged from tears to confusion. The overriding feelings of weariness and futility left me exhausted by the end of each day.

I tried to be obedient, dutiful, and forgiving, but there was precious little joy for me. I tried to behave as a minister of God. People kept watching me, looking for a sign of weakness or failure. I was determined to please the Lord at whatever cost.

I remember that first day when I cleaned Aunt Gerry's apartment. I became overwhelmed by grief while I was dusting a small desk. It had been purchased for Gerry by the then-murdered Rachel. It registered deep within me that I was surrounded with the belongings of the dead. I cried, "Lord, I live in the midst of dead people's things!"

The Lord responded. "Tell Me about your antiques. What are they?" I just had to laugh out loud as I responded to the Lord. "That's what they are, Lord, dead people's things. That's all they are!"

Once again the Lord had given definition to my feelings. He had, with a few words, put the proper perspective on my emotions. So much had happened that my life was, once again, out of my control. He who had created me would have to govern my life and its future. He had taught me to live one day at a time, and with His help I would do it. If there was to be anything more for me then He would have to show me.

God is sovereign, and it was time to not just realize that fact but to live accordingly. Though we sometimes walk through difficult seasons, I have found that it is at His will that we live, and it is at His direction that we move, and it is in His plan that we will find peace. The great stretching sometimes seems unbearable but it is all for our own good. When we yield to Him, then we can live to the glory of God.

chapter 11

LAWYERS AND ACCOUNTANTS

*Now no chastening for the present seemeth to be joyous,
but grievous: nevertheless afterward it yieldeth the peaceable
fruit of righteousness unto them which are exercised thereby.
(Hebrews 12:11)*

 I had scheduled appointments with my lawyer and accountant for the same day. They were sister and brother in Christ and I knew they had my best interests at heart. They had been selected by Bill to serve our family. I felt a real sense of security being in their care. Our lawyer had been our friend for a number of years. She had also been a staunch friend of the ministry, so she had knowledge of most of our problems. I did not know our accountant very well. However, he and Bill watched as our finances had dwindled away, so I knew he was very much aware of our situation. I knew that God would give them wisdom on my behalf, but I was not one bit prepared for their news.

I met with our lawyer first. We discussed many things. Doubt had been cast on the validity of my claim for Bill's life insurance. In response to her letters, it seems the insurance companies were denying existence of "said policies." They were also questioning whether Bill had paid the number of premiums which would have been required. The news was disturbing but it did not hold the highest position on my emotional priority list. The possibility that I was penniless, and would continue to be so, would have to take its place in line. Surviving financially had nowhere near the importance of surviving emotionally.

I knew that she was concerned for me but was compelled as my lawyer to lay out some realistic, though bitter, truths. I had no money and it didn't look as if I was going to get any. When she finished speaking her concerns to me, she concluded with a short pain-filled statement. She said, "Jane, you must close the bookstore and the ministry! You can't afford to keep them in operation. That's the bottom line." I felt it as a blow to my solar plexus and all strength went out of me. I just sat there listening to her speak about the financial realities of my life.

I thought back for a moment. Bill and I knew that we were to open the ministry. We had heard the voice of God and we were obedient to Him. He had demonstrated His faithfulness over and over. We also knew that we were to open the bookstore. Luke 4:18 Christian Bookstore had been the will of God. We knew that the Lord was in the very center of both projects.

I have noticed that the Body of Christ is often mistaken, believing that the will of God is some kind of panacea to be taken against the storms in life. Sometimes it seems man's version of God is that He is just a larger version of himself. Man thinks that God thinks as he does. Nothing could be further from the truth. Man is created in God's image, not the reverse. Man's abilities, thoughts, and plans are laughably insignificant in comparison. The truths of God are greater than the thoughts of men. I told myself that the facts which we were now considering in the lawyer's office, though overwhelming, were still nothing more than the facts of mere mortals. I loved this woman and I respected her abilities, but I left her office with a sinking feeling in the pit of my stomach.

I drove to the accountant's office with my lawyer's words still ringing in my ears. I found the same message issuing forth from the accountant. Though I did not know him very well, Bill had trusted his judgment and so I was determined to trust him as well. He explained in some detail our financial situation. Though Bill and I still held some real estate in Michigan and Florida, we were cash poor. We lived only on Bill's Social Security check. All our other resources were gone, into the ministry in obedience to God, but nevertheless gone. The picture from his point of view looked grim. He clearly understood our commitment to Christ and my desires to continue in the work. But he could not in good conscience agree with me. He strongly suggested that I must close the bookstore and the ministry. His figures didn't lie. I just didn't have the money to continue in the work. I had heard from both of them; though they were both believers they said the same thing. They said that I must close down a sovereign work of God. They had told me what I must do, but what of God? What would He say?

As I drove back to Gerry's apartment, which had become my "Elijah's cave", the tears came. I thought about the bookstore and the ministry. Both had begun with such promise and joy. I knew that through the years we had made mistakes but God had been quick to correct us and repair any damage we had caused. God had been faithful to the ministry and also to the bookstore. We had been through trying times, but I hated to give everything up. Was it just my pride, I wondered? I hoped not, but whatever God said I would do. I had told both the lawyer and the accountant that I would pray and would try to find the will of God. Much as I appreciated everything that they had told me, I would do what the Lord said.

It was now just two months since Bill had gone to be with the Lord. Nothing came easily. Everything had been turned upside down and much of my life seemed to be in ruin. It was all a great struggle and I knew the enemy was toying with my mind and my emotions. I didn't know how much more of it I could take. At times, strength ran through me like water through a sieve. I would be left weak and disoriented. I could think of no one who would be willing to come alongside to help, willing to be poured out daily in this work. Was I to give the ministry to someone else? What was I to do?

I walked in despair, worked in despair, and lived in despair. There seemed no way out of this trial. I could not go backward and return to easier times. And having just heard from my two close advisers, I could not go backward or forward. I was stuck.

My thoughts wandered to the ministry. Bill's stamp was on it and the place was full of him. His books, his pictures, even his scent remained. I do not know how many times I looked to his chair for a response as I ministered in his office. A shadow would pass my eye and I would look up expecting to see him. A sound in the building would bring momentary hope that it could be Bill. I was surrounded by him, but miserably, I was without him.

It was difficult at best to work under these conditions but returning to my "cave" was not much easier. The stairs kept getting steeper and my surroundings became even more somber. Everything began to look like I felt - dull, uninteresting, and filled with painful memories. Gerry's furniture was old and badly in need of repair. The apartment took on the drab look of her belongings and it agreed with my spirit. Everything around me seemed unhappy also. There was very little in my daily life which gave me pleasure, joy, peace, or purpose. This world had nothing I wanted. What I wanted was in another world, another time, and another space. There was nothing here in my daily life to draw me into the joy of life and I took no pleasure in this world.

Often when I sought refuge from the storms of life, I would come to the foot of our bed and drop to my knees. I would then petition God. My body might drag into the bedroom, but as my lips would form the first words of praise then His spirit would begin to bubble up on the inside of me. I would begin to feel the day's problems lift from me and my prayers could increase. I would often lay my head on the foot of my bed and weep. I would begin with a sorrowing heart, but as God would encourage me then my tears would come from a thankful heart.

God had not left me. I was not totally alone. As I would cry out to God, then the brutalizing thoughts and fears would pass and the assurance of God would flood my soul. I was reminded that we are tri-part beings—spirit, soul and flesh.

Our spirits, our only eternal part, having been touched by God give us passage into His very presence. That is how we hear His voice. It is the voice of the Holy Spirit that we hear; He gives us God's direction and His peace.

God speaks often of the soul. In fact, I have found that the Bible holds over 500 scriptures pertaining to the soul. Our bodies are only mentioned about 170 times. Things spiritual, on the other hand, are discussed in about 600 scriptures. It is easy to see the importance that God places on our souls and our spirits. Soulish things have a significant impact upon humanity. All too often we attribute our problems to the devil. In fact many of our troubles are not caused by outside forces, but they are the direct result of our own behavior and value systems.

During times of grief, there is a definite tearing away within our bodies. Separating our soul from our flesh and spirit. Our spirits can sometimes be in agreement with God, while our souls can be in total disagreement. We struggle against Him and His will. In these times of inner conflict and struggle our bodies can be ill-affected and we can suffer in the physical realm as a result of the battle. As our bodies suffer, so do our souls, and we feel that we are overwhelmed and in chaos.

My daily coming into agreement with God took dogged determination in the difficult task of personally yielding to God. Though that statement might appear contradictory, it is not. It was in the determination to be yielded to God, no matter the cost, that the ultimate victory over my soul could be won. Grief could assault my soul, causing a lengthy inward look and in doing so affect my health and my spiritual well-being. It soon became apparent to me that only by yielding to God's will and plan over my desires and plans could I sufficiently conquer my enemy and gain the key elements I needed for victory.

Well-meaning people quoted scriptures to me, but they did little good. I was already aware of the scriptures. My great war would not be won by patching on a scripture here and there. This war could be won only by yielding to and agreeing with God, just as Jesus had done in the Garden of Gethsemane. Those were the Scriptures that gave me help. As the Lord was strengthened, so was I. As He walked in obedience, so must I.

I was in this frame of mind when I returned to my apartment that day after consultation with the lawyer and accountant.

I closed the door on the world and walked woodenly to my bedroom. I dropped to my knees and released my emotions. Tears, groans, and sobbing cries escaped from me. I cried until I could cry no more. I fell exhausted against the foot of my bed. I could only whimper like a child.

Then I became angry with myself. How could I have allowed such soulish emotions to break forth from me? I began to pray in earnest. I called out for forgiveness, for I had let self-pity enter and I had become its victim. I had approached the throne of God in defeat and had carried all my self-pity with me. My mind knew what my emotions would not accept. God was sovereign and His Word was true. His Word promised that He would never leave me nor forsake me, no matter how difficult my situation. The sweet little Scriptures, which people had spoken to me in kindness, now sprang to my lips in praise. I confessed my sin and asked God for His will and His plan. "What do you want me to do, Lord?" I cried out. "What is Your will for me? What about the bookstore and the ministry? Lord, you have heard the words of men today concerning my future, but what would you have me do?"

Peace flooded me, all parts of me. My spirit, flesh, and soul. I was flooded with the peace of God as I heard Him say, in declaration: "You can accept the words of men, close the bookstore and the ministry and live the rest of your days on your finite resources. Or you can take My hand, trust Me, keep the bookstore and the ministry in operation, and live out the rest of your days on My infinite resources. You must decide."

God had spoken, I had heard Him and my decision was made. I spoke aloud, so that all could hear, whether they were visible or invisible. I, too, would make a declaration: "I will take your hand, trust you, and I will follow your directions." I was surprised at my boldness when I said to Him, "Lord, please consider me as your date for the duration."

After a time of rest in His presence, I got up to call my lawyer and my accountant. I gave them the news, that I would keep the bookstore and the ministry in full operation. Everything would stay the same as long as God gave me strength. I would trust God for His provision. I gave them the opportunity to agree or to disagree that I had heard the Lord. They both agreed to continue with me. I thank God for them, and they take an important place in my prayer life. God used them to bring me to Him and to seek His wisdom for my future. God gave me an option, and I chose God!

chapter 12

RANCH PROPERTY

When a man's ways please the LORD,
he maketh even his enemies to be at peace with him.
(Proverbs 16:7)

Many years before Disney changed Florida, we had bought some unimproved property in east central Florida. We leased our land to some adjacent cattle ranchers and enjoyed certain tax benefits. As long as the land was used in this way, the property was considered agricultural and we would receive certain tax considerations.

In 1990, our son John had decided to try his hand at raising some range cows. He had approached us with this proposition and we had agreed. We agreed to lease him the land for $1.00 a year, so we put the property in his hands. This agreement seemed satisfactory but some months later we received a letter from the property appraiser's office. It appeared that we had run afoul of some of their rules and they were informing us of the impending loss of our agricultural status.

Bill was surprised. John and his partner had worked very hard putting up fences, clearing land, and building a road. They had studied hard and soon became quite knowledgeable about raising range cattle. Their herd was small but they had plans to steadily increase its size as money for expansion was made available.

A few months before he died Bill had made an appointment with the Seminole County Property Appraisers to fight their claim. They were contending that we had no bona fide cattle business. Though our son John's efforts were small, Bill felt that their charges should be challenged. He had made an appointment to appeal. We were concerned, wondering if we could afford to keep this property if the county was successful in disapproving our agricultural classification. This was a beautiful piece of property. We had bought it as an investment when the land was relatively cheap. Land values had increased considerably so we were obliged to fight this decision. We could no longer afford to keep the land without the agricultural benefit.

After receiving the letter from the county agents, Bill spent hours at the library. He researched the tax laws and returned home tired but satisfied that the county was wrong. His only comment was, "Nowhere in the law does it mention the number of cattle that you must have to be declared a cattle ranch." Since I was not directly involved with the challenge, I paid little attention and asked no questions.

I had forgotten all about this challenge, as my thoughts were on surviving Bill's death. It was rudely brought to my attention, however, upon receipt of a letter from the Seminole County Appraisers. They were notifying Bill that a date had been set for his challenge. The letter was short and to the point. My heart sank as I realized that I had but a few short weeks to prepare.

I was so tired of all these battles. Large and small, they came against me relentlessly. If things could go wrong, they did, whether at home, at the bookstore, and at the ministry. Everywhere I turned I was under attack. Insurance companies, freezers, leaky roofs, air-conditioners, toilets, electrical ballasts, and parking lot potholes; it was a never-ending struggle. I was at my wits' end.

I asked my home church to pray and to receive a word from the Lord. During the prayer Hazel received a vision. She had clearly seen, in the Spirit, the devil making a smoke screen and then he would paint on it the disaster of his choosing. If I accepted it as real, then it would become real. If, however, I would instantly deny the trouble and rebuke the enemy, then it would disappear like smoke.

In my weariness, I had neglected to take the proper spiritual authority over my circumstances. I had developed the bad habit of persevering and plodding on, through each difficult situation. God wanted me to have victory, but I only wanted to get through it and get to the other side. His patience with me was endless.

At best, it was difficult to praise Him. My heart was still broken and my spirit very wounded. However, I learned.

One evening, while listening to the glorious sounds of those in worship in the ministry sanctuary, I was on my knees bailing out a toilet in the bathroom. I learned the hard way that no matter how difficult my situation, I was expected to be thankful and praise Him. It was a time of pure frustration! Tears came quickly at such times. These situations are designed by the devil to be difficult, tiresome, and spirit-breaking. And they are if we let them be.

I came to understand, however, that no matter how tired I was or how overwhelmed with grief, God would prevail if I would take the proper authority over my situations. It was directly related to the speed with which I rebuked Satan and the speed with which I praised God. The daily disasters which were coming against me did not have to overcome me. I had authority over a great deal more than I was willing to exercise.

I was in the midst of learning this lesson when the letter from the Seminole County Property Appraiser's office arrived. I was determined to practice what I had been taught against the forces that would try to deny us our rights. Bill had believed that we were in the right. I would stand in agreement with that and ask the Lord to be on my side. I felt that I had to at least try. John and I kept the appointment that was meant for Bill, but in truth we were woefully unprepared.

Though unprepared in the natural, I believed God and hoped that He would work a wonder on our behalf. I believed that He would do what I could not, if I would but stand on His Word. It was a trial I did not want to face.

It covered an area in which I was ignorant. Everything seemed to be against us and I was weary of fighting. I had been in a continuous battle since Bill's death and I really didn't think I could stand much more. I lived one day at a time because everything down the road seemed overwhelming. I felt so alone, even with the Lord on my side. Alone, uncovered, unprotected, and vulnerable, that's exactly how I felt. I struggled against my feelings, trying to believe God. I felt one way but God's Word said the truth was the other way. When I felt alone, God's Word said He would never leave me. When I felt uncovered, God's Word said that He would cover me. When I felt unprotected and vulnerable, God's Word said that He would protect me and would take all my burdens. **My greatest battle was to not accept how I felt, but believe the Word of God.**

John and I faced our accusers in a cramped room in the Seminole County Services Building. A woman presided as master, or judge. A woman lawyer represented the county and the only other person in the room was the gentleman from the Property Appraiser's office. He was the young man Bill had been dealing with. He looked surprised when John and I entered the room, and he asked about Bill. I had taken a copy of Bill's death certificate with me. I knew that if I were put in the position of having to speak about Bill's death in this hostile environment, then I would break down and weep. I slid the death certificate across the table to him, and he appeared sincerely sorry. I accepted his condolences and the fight was on.

The master explained that she would make her decision later and that we would receive the results by mail, in about two weeks. During the hearing, if we had any questions or challenges, we were to raise our hands. She would then decide who would have the floor to speak. The county would make its case and then we would be given time to make our case. There would be a time for argument, summation, and rebuttal. The judge then asked if we had any questions and I said, "I don't think so." I offered a silent prayer but nothing had prepared us for what was to come next.

Venomous accusations came against us. We were accused of trying to defraud the county of its rightful tax revenue. The charges and the lawyer's fervor amazed me. The attorney painted a picture that was abhorrent to me. She spoke of Bill as if he had willfully lied and cheated the county government by deceitful and underhanded means. I was flabbergasted. Her words were bitter and accusing. Though she had never met him, she spoke about Bill in a harsh and cruel manner. It was a hard thing to hear.

In my mind, I kept calling out to Jesus. "Help us, Jesus, help us. Give us wisdom. Oh Lord, help us."

She continued to speak to the judge about Bill's intent to defraud. "Your Honor," she said. "He only charged his son $1.00 a year for the land, which is evidence that there was no intent to have a cattle business."

My hand shot up and the judge nodded to me. "Where, Your Honor, is it written that a man can't help his son?" I asked.

"Nowhere," she responded.

The attorney for the county went on. "There are discrepancies in the books, Your Honor," she said. "The son has a receipt for a truck and he's entered it twice."

John raised his hand and the judge nodded to him. "Please show me," John asked. "We don't own a truck. There should be no receipts for a truck."

The attorney impatiently shoved over to him two receipts dated weeks apart. She continued to imply that we were lying to the taxing authorities. John quietly got to his feet and reached across the table. He showed the receipts to the judge. "Your Honor," he said, "these are receipts for a tractor. The first one represents the down payment and the other represents the final payment." He continued, "I know that my books are not the best, but believe me, there is no intent to defraud, lie, or deceive."

The attorney was not finished. She again attacked us. She said the land was not being fully utilized, indicating that we used poor farming practices.

Again, my hand went up, "Your Honor," I said, "my husband and I never agreed with the practice of the total use of the land. Part of the property that the county is talking about is a water reclamation area. Though we own 140 acres, 40 of them are swampy. We have fought to protect the wetlands and its wildlife for years. I believe that it's good land management to protect the wet area. John is only using the remaining 100 acres for his cattle." I stopped to catch my breath, amazed at my boldness. "Your Honor," I continued, "the county has said that we don't have enough cattle on the land, and their claim is based on the full 140 acres. If they would reduce the usable land to 100 acres, then their assessment might be more realistic."

Again I stopped for breath. "In response to the county's claim about the number of cattle," I said, "I am reminded of the one remark that my husband made after he had spent hours in research into the matter. He said that nowhere in the law was he able to find any figures pertaining to what constituted a cattle operation. He was quite adamant about it, Your Honor."

The lawyer was quick to respond. "That's correct, it is not written in the body of the law. We rely on 'the folk' to tell us the numbers of cattle that the land can support."

In unison John and I responded, "The folk?" We were amazed at hearing this incredible statement. It might have been good usage for them but all we could envision was the little "wee people" from fairy tale land. We laughed and the attorney became flustered and angry.

The county agent, who had remained silent throughout the proceedings, finally spoke. "We rely on the wisdom from such groups as the Cattlemen's Association to give us direction. Their research shows us the best possible use of the land and how many head a parcel can sustain at maximum use."

Again my hand went up in the air. "I have already addressed the subject of maximum use. My husband and I never agreed to the depletion of the land by overuse. This is a special piece of property and it has a delicate ecological system. We intend to do our best to keep it balanced. God has given us the land, and we are to take care of it, but not abuse it. We have always appreciated that John was careful to accommodate our feelings in this matter."

The judge noticed that John had brought some pictures. My son-in-law, who was a lawyer, had suggested that judges like to see the land that is under contention. John had gone out to the property and taken a roll of pictures. He photographed some of the improvements that had been made, the water troughs that he had built, the fencing that he had installed, and his cattle. He was quick to show her the pictures and to explain each one. She had some questions for him, and I was quite impressed with his knowledge of the care and feeding of range cattle. Even the county agent had to nod in agreement as John explained the use of molasses, as an aid to their digestion.

As John and the judge were talking, I looked out of the small window behind the judge's chair. I sensed the presence of an angel. I had no idea of the outcome of this battle, but I knew that I was not in it alone.

We all sat quietly for a moment and the judge spoke. She said, "I have made my decision and I will render it now. I am deciding for you and against the county." She pointed at John. "My decision is very close. Do a better job," she said, as she closed the files and set them aside.

My knees were weak and I glanced again at the window. My friend from heaven was still there and he had caused men's hearts to change. As John and I walked to the car, I commented with a smile when I noticed his choice of parking places. "John, the last time Daddy and I were here," I said, "He parked in the exact same spot." When we got into the car, I told John about the scripture that the Lord had given me just that morning - Proverbs 16:7, *"When a man's ways please the Lord, He maketh even his enemies to be at peace with him."*

John looked at me and smiled a very small smile. "God sure did it for us, Mom," he said. "He sure did."

On the drive home, I praised the Lord. I thanked him for His faithfulness. We had been told by everyone that we could not win this case. We were only a mother and a son against the entire county government. But holding fast to the truths of God, we had been victorious. Once again I experienced the presence of the Lord in the very center of the struggle. We had been like the three Hebrew children in the fiery furnace. One greater than they walked with them, and today He walks with us.

chapter 13

The First Year

And we know that all things work together
for good to them that love God,
to them who are the called according to his purpose.
(Romans 8:28)

Endless battles continued to rage about me. They were the plans of Satan, designed and engineered to demoralize and frighten me. His intent was for my total resignation from the army of faith.

I sometimes thought about Satan. I was amazed at his tenacity and often wondered if he too became frustrated. His plans were always being altered, and then used by God for the strengthening of the saints, eventually to defeat the devil. Scripture tells us that God causes all things to work together for good to those who love him. That must be a discouraging word for the devil, to forever have all his best efforts turned for good in the life of the believer. Of course, the outcome depends upon our willingness to trust God, even in the darkest hours.

I knew that truth before Bill's death, as we had often been required to stand against the works of the enemy.

Many times we rejoiced together in God's victories. Now
I was being taught to stand alone with God and I hated
it. I spent many sleepless hours on my bed of tears. I
complained bitterly against God's plan for my life. Any
plan which excluded Bill was no plan for me. I was happy
for Bill. He was with God and that was wonderful. For him
it was wonderful, but it was not wonderful for me. I was
unhappy that we had been separated and I had been left
behind. It seemed the worst kind of betrayal.

The Lord would speak to me, to comfort and inform,
but I would often just shake my head in disagreement
with Him. He spoke often of the "new beginning" for
me, but I was not interested. I had not yet completely put
down the old. Every day I tried to let go of Bill. I tried
to be obedient but we had been forged together and it
was brutally hard to let go. I continued in my private
agonies, mostly at night while alone. Almost every day
new troubles would surface. Almost every night I would
struggle against my situation.

In the beginning, my struggles were directly with Satan,
the enemy of God. In my dreams he would come to gloat
over his victory, always insisting that he had won and
that Bill was with him. I would awaken startled, my heart
pounding in fear over these evil disclosures. It would take
some time to erase the memories of these dreams and to
wipe his filthy lies from my mind. As I cried out to the Lord
He would be there to comfort me and to speak truth to me:
Bill was with Him. I would then awaken to be happy for

his new life, and thankful that he was free and filled with everlasting joy in our Lord.

By day Satan would come and bring doubt to my mind. Had I mishandled Bill's last illness? If I had only made him stay in the hospital instead of letting him come home. The phrase, "if I had only" haunted me day and night. It defiled me and filled me with feelings of guilt. Could I have done more? Should I have done it differently? The questions came, piercing my very soul.

For years, during Bill's alcoholism, I had typically taken on the responsibility for his drinking. It was a mistake then, and now I found myself doing exactly the same thing. I was picking up the responsibility for Bill's death. His death came so suddenly, and my faith in God's deliverance was so sure, that my soulish parts became bound in turmoil. Had I missed God? Did I not hear Him properly when He gave me John 17:15 to stand on? Doubt, mistakenly-assumed guilt, and weariness, coupled with the daily responsibilities of keeping the ministry in operation, besieged me.

I would often develop a "circle the wagons" mentality, and I would isolate myself from the rest of the world. I kept only my family close to me. It seemed that no one else really understood me and what I was going through. Unless they had experienced a similar loss, they didn't seem to comprehend. I might look fine on the outside but inside I was in turmoil. I wanted to yell when people would say to me, "You're handling this so well, my dear." I really wanted to scream at them and ask, "Can't you see me, really see what's going on inside of me? The pain, the turmoil, the grief, can't you see it? Are you blind to my true condition?" But quietly, with these thoughts unspoken, I would return to the comfort of my place in God's wings. Then I would accept again that only He really understood, and that no other person could fill the void and loss that was in my heart.

Conventional wisdom foolishly declares that the first year is the hardest, and that everything after that gets easier and easier. That is absurd. I know women whose husbands have been with the Lord for many years, yet just a mention of a special day or time could bring them to tears. We can't put time limits on our emotions.

We are all made by God, but we are all made differently. None of us is exactly the same physically, so why should we be expected to be the same emotionally? Even the church has developed some worldly habits in its assumptions about grief and suffering. This causes bad counsel and leaves the bereaved uncertain about their spiritual well being. The story is told about Jesus seeking solitude upon hearing of the death of John the Baptist. If Jesus needed time apart with God, so shall we!

The first year is filled with "first anniversaries", and our friends and acquaintances breathe a sigh of relief as we cross over that imaginary threshold. What people don't seem to understand in many instances is that we have prepared ourselves for the "first anniversaries". We have been dreading them and we have steeled our hearts to survive those special days. Bill especially disliked large crowds and manufactured fun, so we seldom went to the Central Florida theme parks. Because there would be no memories there, that's where I spent my first wedding anniversary without him. I made a geographic change and carefully avoided painful memories.

It's the little things, the surprises that overwhelm us. They sneak up behind us, grab our heart in a tight grip, and we "crash and burn." A surprise phone call, or a letter from a far-away friend who is not aware that our beloved is gone, these things can set us off. Seeing someone in traffic that for a brief moment resembles our beloved, digs deep into our soul. We are not prepared for the surprises on our third anniversary, or our sixth, or our twentieth. We must not lose sight of the true meaning of marriage. We have been bound to this man, flesh, soul, and spirit, for years. In our cleaving together we have become one, and once that oneness is cut away, then only God knows our pain and only God can minister to our pain, a pain that cuts across flesh, soul, and spirit.

It is preposterous to set goals and arbitrary deadlines on healing. No one can tell how quickly we will heal, or define the occasion which will cause us to grieve. Every day has its own problems and pitfalls. The Book of Matthew, in the 6th chapter and the 34th verse, puts it this way: *"Take therefore no thought for the morrow; for the morrow shall take thought for the things of itself. Sufficient unto the day is the evil thereof."*

We should neither set boundaries, nor have false expectations. Nor should those who love us expect a magic deliverance from grief within the confines of one year. So much depends upon our relationship with God, our relationship with our loved one, the kind of marriage that we had, and the number of years that we spent together. It also includes the length of time of his illness, and the conditions of our own mind and spirit. Was death sudden or was it a long and difficult time, filled with pain for all concerned? All these things and more work together to build the time of mourning, severely impacting its duration.

Some things are easier than we expect, and some things are much harder. Laughing alone was, for me, one of the great surprises. Bill and I were great companions and we laughed together often. I was very surprised when I learned by experience that a solitary chuckle has a hollow sound. When there is no one to share a joke it seems strange and lonely, as if it also aches for a friend.

I could no longer watch football games on TV. Bill and I had been great fans, loudly rooting for our favorites. We would share popcorn and cheer for the team. I could no longer watch; it only made me miss him more acutely. The death of a loved one changes life, and old habits must fall away for a time until we adjust to new surroundings. A letter from an acquaintance would often bring me to tears.

Though they were well-meant, some condolences seemed as salt to an open wound.

My battle against the insurance companies took almost a year to resolve. They finally paid, but they fought a desperate battle with delaying tactics and paper chases. When Bill purchased the insurance in the early years of our marriage, he explained that life insurance was to pay death expenses. It was also to be a foundation on which the widow could build a new life. Life insurance is a poor investment for monetary gain but its purpose was for funding those difficult times immediately following death.

If the Lord had not made the arrangements to sell our home so quickly, I would have had no money on which to live. Men have decided that widows should not make any major decisions until they have lived through the first year of widowhood. That is absolutely ludicrous. Before leaving our beloved's deathbed, we are forced to make major decisions.

Generally speaking, the basic decisions about the body of the deceased have been made at a much earlier time. In those impromptu talks which follow the sudden death of a friend, we freely discuss our preferences and a basic foundation is set. But we can't possibly be prepared for our emotional state immediately following death. If we have not made plans for donating organs, it's a troubling shock when we are immediately approached by hospital personnel for our loved one's body parts. The donor program is a good one; however, if it has not been discussed and we are not prepared for the speed with which the organs must be taken after death, it is a great shock. We can't just say, "I am not prepared to make a big decision for at least a year." I was reminded again that men's wisdom is filled with foolishness. On the other hand, God has wisdom, all that we will ever need.

Contrary to many reports, I had no long wait for the Social Security System to respond to my need. The Lord arranged for me to receive the widow's benefit from Bill's Social Security. He gave me a wonderful young man on the telephone who quickly processed all the paper work. Within a little over a week after making application, I started to receive my checks. By selling the house so quickly, I was well able to make the few remaining payments on Aunt Gerry's condominium.

Literally within weeks I had a place to live and Social Security checks for a monthly income. The tithe from the sale of our home fed the ministry, enabling the ministry to pay its bills.

Because my husband in his spiritual path was a tither, that is a practice I determined to maintain. I found many good books on the subject. It is very important to know that God expects us to be faithful to Him if we are expecting Him to be faithful to us. The word "tithe" means a tenth part which is to be set aside for the work of the Kingdom. Pastors or other church leaders can give guidance in this matter. Following God's wisdom in tithing, as in all aspects of our walk with Him, will provide a solid foundation. I learned, and share here, that provision for my future depended upon my obedience.

God had once again done the impossible and through my willingness to believe Him and trust Him, He had moved on my behalf. From the throne room of God I heard Him say that, "I have just begun to work on your behalf." He also said, "Bill was a good husband to you and good provider, however, I will be a better one."

• • •

If you have never made the decision to turn your life into His hands, now is the time. If you are reading this book and have ever wondered about the reality of Christ, you could make no better decision than to turn to Him right now. It takes little effort on your part. You are likely already broken, or you wouldn't be reading this book. Stop and call out to Him. You need no set prayer, just call out for help. If you have lived without giving yourself to Him, then you have undoubtedly sinned. Ask Him to forgive you for your sins, then give your heart to Jesus. Ask Him to come into your heart, and He will. He will fill your heart and be your Savior. Give Him your whole life, and He will become your Lord. Give your tears, sorrow, and grief to Him, and He will hold you and comfort you. Ask Him to fill you by His Spirit, and He will do it. Once you are filled with the Spirit of God, you shall have the strength you need to confront the rest of your life.

chapter 14

THE "NEW BEGINNING"

Submitting yourselves one to another in the fear of God.
(Ephesians 5:21)

God tells us to give thanks for all things. That includes: good or evil, easy or difficult, a "piece of cake" or a challenge. Driving Aunt Gerry's car was both difficult and challenging. It had been a trial for Bill and now it was a trial for me.

Before Bill died a problem had arisen with the ignition. The keys had frozen solidly into the ignition and it became impossible to remove them from the steering column. No matter how hard Bill tried, he was unable to disconnect the keys from the car.

The car was a rusty old "clunker". Gerry had only driven it to the grocery store, the bank, and to her few appointments. It spent most of its life in "park". She had lived in a small condominium on the ocean in Palm Beach, so the car sat uncovered and open to the salt air. It became our only transportation and we were grateful for it.

Legally the car still belonged to Rachel since she had changed the ownership on the registration just before her savage death. Her attorney, however, was not interested in adding a rusty old Chevrolet to her list of assets. Without her signature we were unable to return ownership to Gerry, nor could she legally give us the car. Gerry told Bill, "Drive it till it drops."

One quick look suggested that the "drop dead" time could be just around the next corner.

Most automobiles run on petroleum products. This one ran on a mixture of gas and prayer. We would fill the tank with gas, keep a watchful eye on the oil consumption, but it was robust prayer and praise which kept the car in operation. Bill felt that we could drive this beauty until the Lord provided the resources to buy a newer car. As long as Bill was around, the car posed no immediate problem, but when death intervened, I was left with this rusty challenge.

While driving this car it was never difficult to be thankful. If I arrived at my destination, I was thankful. I could not go anywhere without a deep sense of thanksgiving to God and the forces that He had set about me to protect and direct my path.

A couple we knew owned the local Exxon station in our neighborhood. They had become friends through the work at the ministry. I know that they were filled with apprehension every time I drove this troublesome car into their station. The car was not worth the time nor money for drastic repairs, so all we could do was to hold it together until the Lord moved.

Little things continued to plague the car. Our friend would patiently examine the problem area, and shake his head. He would deftly "jury rig" a fix, and explain again the ramification of each new problem. He was filling me with knowledge which I had hoped I would never need. He would end each automotive discourse with, "You need to buy a better car."

I surely wanted a better car but the Lord had not yet opened that door and I learned to be thankful for that which I had. Every time that I went for gas, it seemed uncanny but a new problem would arise. He would patch it or show me another way around it. There was little else that I could do. I continued to be grateful and to thank the Lord for the transportation which He had provided.

God kept the car running but rust and age had done its work. One hot day while driving in Orlando the air-conditioning quit, never to go again. Being without air-conditioning just accentuated a larger overall problem. The internal controls for the windows were rusted through. We could only open the windows part way. For example, the window on the driver's side opened but a scant three inches, which made toll paying very inconvenient. If I forced the window to open wider, making it easier to breathe, then I could not close it against the rain.

The speedometer cable had broken long ago so I never knew my speed. No matter how fast I went, the needle stayed stubbornly below -0- miles per hour. The next large thing to break was the parking gear. I could not put the car in park. The hand brake gave out at the same time, making each parking experience a real challenge. The solution seemed easy enough, though the doing was tricky.

First, I learned to look for the flattest parking place available. Then I would slowly coast into it. Next, I would press the brake pedal and come to a stop. I would then put the gear shift in "neutral" and hop out of the car. Trying to get out of the way of the car door I would quickly place a short piece of two-by-four under the tire. The tire I chose would depend on the slant of the lot. I became quite proficient in judging which would be the best. If I was blessed enough to find a lot with concrete bumpers and if the lot drained in the right direction then I could bring the car to rest against the bumpers and rejoice.

I also became accomplished in putting the wood under the tires. In high heels or in flat shoes, the dance was always the same. If I could accomplish all of it without any injury to life and limb, I considered myself blessed. I was grateful for each and every victory. Life can get very exciting when just the act of parking a car takes on such drama. Upon leaving the parking lot, the routine was just reversed - to be done again at my next stop and the next and the next.

One day as I pulled into a hardware store the entire bottom structure of the driver's door fell out on the pavement. It took with it most of the working parts. For a moment I just sat there looking at the mess and forgetting to be grateful.

The Lord reminded me, so with great ceremony and thanksgiving, I scooped up all the rusty parts and put them in the trunk. I don't know why I kept the insides of the door but I really didn't know what else to do with them.

I hope I am conveying a true picture of this car. It began life dressed in shiny white. Rust and weather had streaked it to "a dappled car of many colors". The underside of the carriage was wired in place with the muffler and the tailpipe hanging precariously low, almost touching the ground.

The keys still stubbornly refused to budge from the ignition. Since Bill's death, however, I had taken to hanging a copy of Billy Graham's Decision magazine over the steering column. I figured that if any one wanted to steal this beauty, then they would have to get by Graham and make a different decision than the one he was calling for. Gerry had an extra key so I was at least able to lock the doors.

The upholstery had faded to a genteel gray. The headliner sagged so badly that I could not see out of the rear window. I rolled, stapled and pinned it. I made pleats and folds in order to see, but the material was so rotten that I was continually forced to repair my work. When I would drive along slowly, with the wind whistling through the partially opened windows, it would cause the headliner to undulate rhythmically and all the pins and staples would click together like miniature castanets. The song from the muffler would join the chorus, adding a sound very much like sheep in distress. The car sang its song and I sang mine; we made a noise that only God could love. With the appearance mixed with the sound of the car, it gave off a kind of gypsy quality in which only the most venturesome would dare to ride.

When the car was at rest with its sagging underbelly, it always held the telltale two-by-four, pressed against its wheels. With the position of the two-by-four determined by my location and my dexterity, sometimes the angles of placement were stylish and sometimes they were just plain utilitarian.

I would ask the Lord about a better car and He would tell me to be thankful for what I had. He would say, "In My perfect timing I will deliver what you need. Have a thankful heart for that which I have given you." So that was my life, always in search of flat parking places, praying every mile, and blessing God with a thankful heart.

One evening Katherine called with a surprise. She and John had inherited some money and they wanted to buy me a car. John had suggested it and they made plans to join forces to split the cost. They wanted to give me safer transportation. I quickly rejected their kind offer. After all, I was the mother. Bill and I had bought their first cars and I was not comfortable in receiving. I thanked her but said, "No! If God wants me to have a different car, then He will arrange it." I could not accept their offer. I felt that I would be losing my place as parent and become care-receiver, instead of the care-giver. At times like this roles can often be reversed, and I was being careful that it didn't happen to me. They had their lives to live and I didn't want them saddled with my problems.

As I hung up the phone, I felt the tug of the Holy Spirit and I dropped to my knees to hear God. "Child" He said, "I have put it in your children's hearts to buy you a car. How else could I cause them to tithe the gift which I have given them? By buying you a car My will can be accomplished and then you will put their gift into My work." For years Bill and I had prayed that our children would not only be saved as a part of our household, but would become useful workers in the Kingdom of God. The Lord gently reminded me of all those prayers. I quickly asked His forgiveness and called Katherine. I explained to her that the Lord had told me to accept their generous offer.

After that conversation John called to reaffirm their desire to stand together and get me better transportation. Proverbs 31:28 rang in my ears: Her children rise up and bless her. That is exactly what God had accomplished. My children had wanted to bless me and I had almost let foolish pride stand in the way. It almost caused us all to miss a blessing by denying them an opportunity to be obedient to God.

The big day finally arrived. I was to go to Katherine's for the weekend. My son-in-law would take me car shopping. John would join us later to see the car. I was excited about the prospects of driving a car with conveniences... windows that worked, gear shifts that operated, a speedometer that really showed the speed...and best of all, keys that could be removed. I was also looking forward to my last drive in "Gerry's Jolly Junker".

It would be my last visit to the friendly gas station in this car. It was a time for cheering. The station owners were as eager as I with the prospects of a newer car. He checked the car over one last time and as he closed the hood, the latch fell off. He shook his head in disgust and went off to find something suitable to wire the hood closed for its last trip to Katherine's. They all stood watching as I pulled out into traffic. I don't think they held out much hope for a safe arrival to my destination.

Again prayer saved the day and at the predetermined time I drove into Katherine's driveway. She had prepared a special place under the trees for the car to rest. I crawled out of the driver's seat for the last time and gently patted this faithful friend, saying goodbye. My son John would take care of the final disposition of the car.

Against all odds I had been blessed with transportation. Undesirable as it appeared, it worked for me and was faithful to the last mile. I learned a great deal about life in the "slow lane", and I learned to be grateful in all things.

The prospects of a new car reminded me of how very often the Lord would talk to me about "new beginnings". At first I just didn't want to hear it. As time passed and God continued to heal me, I began to listen. I would be still and listen without argument as He spoke of my future. I remember once asking Him, "Will I recognize the new beginning or will I walk right through it and miss the occasion?"

The issue of the "new beginnings" would be raised every few months. I must admit that my attitude was one of doubt. As I drove to Katherine's, I had hopes that something wonderful would happen, but I was not really anticipating anything. I was coming close to the end of my first year without Bill and I was still wearing "mourning clothes" on my soul.

I was living in obedience, but my life colorless and drab. Everything was hard work. The Lord spoke of joy but I had precious little of it. The Lord spoke of fullness but I felt empty. The Lord spoke of riches but I was poor of spirit. The Lord spoke of strength but I was weak. These were all great promises from God but Bill had died without seeing some of these promises fulfilled in his life here on earth. Would I also? The turmoil of my thought life would always end when I would say to the Lord, "Your will be done Lord, your will be done."

My son-in-law was well-prepared for the great car hunt. He had researched the newspapers and visited some car lots. I wanted a small two-door car. I had always leaned toward the more sporty models, to Bill's chagrin. He was satisfied with the more practical cars, but he usually gave in to me, at least for the car which I would drive. The two of us spent Friday and Saturday looking. We visited every car lot in our path.

Nothing struck us as being just right. We spent hours driving and looking. It was not until late Saturday afternoon that we found the right one. It was a slightly used but perfectly kept Honda Prelude. It had more features than we had agreed on. It was a small two-door car, with air bags, sun roof, automatic shift, power brakes, air conditioning, stereo sound and a tape deck. It was gleaming white and it was beautiful. We took it for a test drive. It was only a year old, had low mileage and it was definitely my car. Everything fit me perfectly. It was more than I could have imagined. Even the price was right. We held the car with a handshake and the few dollars we had in our pockets. We quickly drove home for the checkbook and returned with the entire family. Katherine and the children wanted to see Grammy's new car. Within minutes the deal was made. I was now the owner of a beautiful little car, a gift from my children led by the Holy Spirit. God had once again come through.

Katie and John Palmer rode home with me. John kept busy pushing buttons, playing the radio and requesting that the sun roof be opened. While he was making demands, I heard from heaven. "How do you like your car?" the Lord asked. "I love it Lord, it's just perfect. Thank you, Lord," I said.

"What is the name of your car?" He asked.

"It's a Honda," I answered. "You know that."

"Not the name of the manufacturer, the name of the model?" He asked again.

"Oh, Lord, it's a Prelude," I responded.

"And exactly what does prelude mean?" He asked.

"You know, Lord, it's a beginning." All of a sudden I understood what He was saying. This was it. The new beginning which I had been dreading; instead of hating it, I was loving it.

What fools we are when we argue against God. After all, He does know best and His gifts are always the best.

chapter 15

Marco Island

The sun shall be no more thy light by day;
neither for brightness shall the moon give light unto thee:
but the LORD shall be unto thee an everlasting light,
and thy God thy glory.
(Isaiah 60:19-20)

God, having given me faithful transportation, opened my world to some travel. As He instructed the disciples in Acts 1-8, to go forth from Jerusalem to Judea, Samaria and even to the remotest part of the earth, He also instructed me. My schedule began to include ministry trips outside of my immediate surroundings. Doors were opened from South Florida to South Carolina and parts in between. I met new people and developed new friends. Some of these new friends opened altogether new avenues of ministry for me, and God kept leading the way.

God had been telling me that I would write this book. I had heard it, but I was having difficulty believing it. I'm not a writer. I'm a storyteller. Writing demands a discipline I don't possess, but God kept encouraging me. I received a strong word of confirmation on the occasion of my ordination.

I was ordained in La Grange, Georgia, under the hands of the gifted evangelist, Jimmy Smith. It was one of those spiritual surprises which God loves to engineer on behalf of His children. I had made the trip with an admired friend, the renown artist, Zoe' Mac. She is filled with the Spirit of God and so are her paintings. While in La Grange we had visited a wonderful church. It was an all-black congregation in a country setting in north west Georgia. The service was lively and filled with the Spirit of God. The pastor spoke eloquently that day. I was taken with his earnestness and I whispered to the Lord, "I think he is a trustworthy man and I could believe him, Lord." I had no idea at the time of meeting him that he would play a part in my ordination and this work.

The evening for my ordination came and I was glad to see that pastor in attendance. Many gave prophetic words that night but he spoke most powerfully the word from the Lord. He did not know me or the work that Bill and I had accomplished. However, he described perfectly the work of the ministry with all its spiritual ramifications. It was a lengthy discourse and it was accurate. The Holy Spirit was with him that evening and the qualities that had so impressed me that previous Sunday were evident again.

After the ordination service he made his way over to me and he said, "The Lord tells me that you are to write a book. He is also saying that He has told you, but you do not believe Him. He says that you would believe me."

God had told me to write this book but in truth I felt woefully inadequate. I felt surely He had someone else far more capable than I to do this job. I laughed because the man was absolutely right. I explained to him that God used him to carry the confirmation because I had told God during the Sunday Service that he seemed a trustworthy man.

He smiled at me and said, "Well then, get on with it, sister!"

After my return from Georgia I was talking by phone with my friend in Coral Springs. She relayed her sister's kind offer for the use of their vacation house in Marco Island. They generously loaned me their wonderful house. October was the date that we set, and so I began to make plans for this special time away. A time of rest and recuperation, a time to be alone with God. I was a bit apprehensive but I knew that God would minister to me. He had proven His faithfulness over and over, not just in the written word but by deed and action. He had made a way for me often when there seemed to be no way. Puzzling things would happen but He was always there. He would always put things in the proper perspective and clear my vision.

When the work seemed particularly heavy, He would come alongside to help. When I needed encouragement, He lifted my head. When I needed protection, He covered me and hid me from the world. He had been Father,

Companion, Counselor, but now it was time for Him to become my husband.

While preparing myself for my ordination, I had confided to my traveling companion that I felt much like a bride. Impulsively, she picked a small bouquet of wild flowers and as I got into the car she handed them to me. We drove in silence to Jimmy's. I had become unsettled by the small "bridal bouquet". I was not ready to become a bride, Bill was my husband, and though he was with God, I realized that I still held on to that part of him.

I had released his spirit and his flesh had been taken from me, but I had never released him as husband. He still held that place in my life. Bill was still my husband and he still held that authority over me. God revealed that truth to me in those few seconds when my friend handed me that sweet bouquet. Though he had been gone from me for two years, I still held on to him as my husband. I instantly knew that there was more work to be done but God would have to make the way for my deliverance.

My time in Marco Island was to be that deliverance. This was a special time, appointed by God for a sovereign work. Walls would come down and a Holy bonding would happen. Mourning would have to flee and make room for that which was to come. A new and more wonderful relationship would be built between God and His servant. I was going to Marco Island as a widow. I would leave there as a bride, His bride and a part of His bride, the church. Just like a petal is a part of the overall blossom, He would bring me into a new dimension with Him, and I would be forever changed.

I took very little with me to Marco Island. This was not to be a holiday. I knew that God had work to do, so I traveled lightly. I took my Bible, my Bible tapes and recorder, and my copy of Oswald Chambers' daily devotional, *My Utmost for His Highest.* I took a few changes of clothing and a little food. I knew that it would be a time of fasting and prayer, so I needed little else.

I did not want to be distracted by anyone, so only a few people knew where I was. I was determined to press into God and learn of His will for me. I fasted and prayed. I sang songs to Him in praise. I released my personal prayer language till it filled me and the surrounding area. I was doing the best I could to come into the Holy of Holies. I needed to hear God and I hungered for His touch. I pressed into Him with all my strength and determination. I had the house for thirty days and I was not going to leave without His touch.

During the first three weeks a quiet peace settled over me. I listened to the Bible tapes following along with the Word. I felt His presence but nothing more. Each day when I awakened, I was expectant. Was this to be the day? Would God minister to me today? Would this be the day of deliverance for me? Each night as I lay down to sleep I looked forward to the next day. Each new day would be filled with anticipation. I felt much like a child waiting for the flow from a freshly opened bottle of ketchup. I knew that God would not miss me and I was going to be ready to receive from Him. My spirit was prepared; my soul and my flesh soon followed. I left no room for doubt or disappointment. God had arranged all of this and I was sure that He would complete that which He had begun.

I read and reread the Book of Ruth. It had been a favorite of mine before Bill's death, and once again I found myself reading its pages. I could really empathize with Naomi. She was empty and brokenhearted and so was I. She gathered her life around her, and so did I. I could see many parallels between us. She returned to her country and her family, so did I. When she called herself empty and afflicted by God, I joined with her being in like spirit. She had lost her direction for life and was forced to travel a long way back to her roots. I could only make that sort of trip in the Spirit. My flesh could not go but my spirit could. I, too, drove deeply into God, for the Almighty had also dealt bitterly with me.

Early one morning, just as the dawn was breaking, I heard His voice. "Today is the day, My child," He said, "Today is your day of blessings. Prepare yourself, for today is the day." I thought I was prepared. How was I to prepare myself this time, I wondered. Once again He returned my reading to the Book of Ruth. Contained within the third chapter were the directions for preparation. I read it again and saw God's plan. As I had prepared myself for my ordination, I would prepare myself again. I spent the day fasting and praising Him. I washed my hair and dried it in the sun. I bathed, anointed my body, and cut my nails. I laid out my best clothes and I made myself ready. I took inventory of my life and confessed my sins. I prepared juice and bread for Communion and laid them in the upper room. I returned to the ground floor to finish with my chores. Then I waited on the Lord.

At the appointed hour, as the sun slipped below the horizon and into the Gulf of Mexico, I heard His call. "Come to Me child, all is ready." The resonance of His voice stirred my inner being. "Come to me, now," He said.

I was ready and I climbed the stairs. One foot placed before the other, higher and higher, I climbed to meet with the Lord. I knelt in the middle of the little room, and as my hands opened wide, raised in an offering to Him, I heard my own voice. All day long I had been repeating a litany of confession and I was once again releasing memories to the Lord.

For two years I had been letting go of Bill. In each and every way as the Lord had shown me, I had let go. I had let go of Bill as friend, confidant, and lover. I had let him go as companion, provider, and leader. I had let him go as head of the household, prayer partner and covering. I had let go of him as the other part of me. I had let go in all the conceivable ways in which Bill had held me and in which I had held him. I thought I had done it all until that day in Georgia when God showed me that I had not let go of Bill in the role of husband.

Finally, in that special place and in that special time, I let go of Bill as my husband. I spoke the words that I had not been ready to speak before. I released Bill as my husband. I wept as I said, "Lord, I release Bill. I break the bonds which once joined us and I separate myself from him as my husband." In a fresh rush of tears I repeated my words. I felt a great heaviness lift from me. There had been a breaking deep within me as God separated us. Bill's authority over me as husband was finished.

My days of being submitted to Bill and honoring him as my husband were over. God had ended my marriage physically when He took Bill. He had ended my marriage in the soulish part as He taught me to let go of all the facets of our relationship. Now he was ending my marriage spiritually in a great supernatural move. I had released Bill countless times to God, but I had never released him as my husband and consequently, was still bound to him. I was bound to him in life and now death. God wanted to release me from that bondage with the dead.

One does not come into this easily. It takes time before we are willing to let go of our husband in that special role. There are many women who are in a similar situation. They have released their husband as a man but they have never released their man as husband.

Countless women have struggled with the Biblical references addressing the authority of the husband. They have struggled against the demands of submission. I am not totally at peace with some interpretations about the fleshly confines of these doctrines. I am, however, absolutely positive about the authority of husband.

Whether submission in a marriage has been mastered or not, the authority which a husband has over a wife in God's eyes is basically a spiritual one. There are real natural consequences to a husband's authority. In a proper Biblical relationship, the husband is the head and provider for the wife. He completes her and she completes him. When they are in the correct order they fall under the covering of God.

We are talking here about spiritual authority, given by God at the time of marriage. Whether we knew God or not, He knew us. A husband's authority is part of the basic plan, created before the church, to give proper covering to the bride. God holds all authority over the Bride of Christ, much as the husband holds the authority over his own bride. These are spiritual authorities and must be understood as such. When they are understood in this light they become great gifts from God, elevating the place of wife into the authority of the husband. His authority is for protection and cover, showing the wife godly love and care. It is not to be abused as we have all too often heard.

The spiritual authority held by the husband supersedes all natural laws for the believer. Divorce cannot break it. None of the plans of men are able to break the plan of God. We are bound together unto death. It is spoken in our wedding vows from the very beginning of recorded marriage, vows altered by the plan of man, but unchanged in the heavenlies.

Finally through time and trial we are painfully able to release the authority which our husband has held over us. God will engineer the crushing which will bring it forth. As the wine comes forth with the crushing of the grapes and as the perfume comes forth with the crushing of the blossoms, God's crushing will bring forth the new life from deep within.

As Ruth uncovered the feet of Boaz, I uncovered the feet of the Lord. As she lay down, I lay down. As I lay on the floor in that little glass room, I sang the refrain:

> "Cover me, Oh cover me,
>
> Extend the border of your mantle over me.
>
> Because thou art my nearest kinsman,
>
> Cover me, cover me, cover me."

I felt the Lord. I felt His mantle touch me as I lay at His feet. I felt Him dry my tears and hush my sobs. There was definite pain in the parting but there was also God's peace. I knew that I had been obedient and I lay there quietly for a time, saying goodbye to Bill and all that we had been to each other.

I then took the bread and the cup under a new authority. I had been released as wife to Bill, in order to pick up the authority of being wife to God. As I ate His Flesh and drank His Blood, an even stronger flood of the Holy Spirit filled Me. I knew that I had finally accepted the new authority of Jesus as my husband.

It was dark when I finally came down from the upper room. Night had settled her comfortable quilt over this part of the world. The street lights were casting their yellowish beams, softly illuminating the surrounding area. Houses showed forth their lights as families gathered together. They would be sitting at dinner or relaxing before television sets. The visual comfort of home and hearth was evident. I noticed a sense of peace and well being deep within me.

In the two years since Bill's death, my spirit had remained strong in the Lord. However, my flesh and soul had not. Now my soul had been touched by God and a very deep healing had taken place. The torture of widowhood was at an end. Prospects for a future life lay enticingly ahead. God had done what He said He would do in His Word.

Isaiah 54:4-5, says it best. It is written: *"Fear not; for thou shalt not be ashamed: neither be thy confounded; for thou shalt not be put to shame: for thou shalt forget the shame of thy youth, and shall not remember the reproach of thy widowhood anymore. For thy maker is thine husband; the Lord of hosts is his name; and thy redeemer the Holy One of Israel; the God of the whole earth shall he be called."*

My mourning was finished and I had been touched by God. I had broken foreign authorities away from me. Bill was no longer my husband. He had once held that place in my heart but now he was no longer mine. The vows that we had spoken at our marriage had now been laid bare and broken by the power of God. Though I still cry at those special times, Bill now holds a different place in my heart. I still love him and always will, but he is no longer mine. He is God's, just as I am God's, but we walk in different realms. Someday I will be with him but it will never be as it was.

EPILOGUE

For thou desirest not sacrifice; else would I give it: thou delightest not in burnt offering. The sacrifices of God are a broken spirit: a broken and contrite heart, O God, thou wilt not despise (Psalm 51:16-17).

This is the conclusion of this testimony. This part of the story has been told and we are at its end. Now it is time to take a good hard look at what we have learned. We have taken a peek at some of my life experiences, especially those immediately following Bill's death.

Widowhood is difficult. It is soul-piercing and by its own definition, it is death-defying. The widow's walk is an emotional high wire and at times we feel nudged perilously close to catastrophe. Grief stands ready to shove us off the wire and our balancing skills are almost lost to our weaknesses.

We walk uncharted territory, ever mindful that we have never been this way before. We don't know where we are going and there are times when we don't even know where we have been. The shock of our husband's death, even if it has been anticipated, keeps us off balance. We are often unable to fully accept that death has visited and taken away our most precious part.

At the time of our marriage most of us promise to love, honor, and obey. We keep the scriptures and hold ourselves only for him. As time passes a cleaving takes place and our hearts are fully joined. We give ourselves freely to the other and our eyes look away from the pleasures of the world. We turn inward, to make a home, begin a family and to fulfill our Biblically proclaimed role as keepers of the hearth. As our husband becomes the head, we become the heart of the family. We take our rightful place in society, as wife and then mother.

Our early growing years prepare us for this upcoming role. We face, with anticipation and joy, the prospects of falling in love with the right man, marrying him, and becoming his wife. The yearned for day finally arrives and we become his other part, coming under his cover physically, emotionally, and spiritually.

In a more gentle time society prepared us for marriage, home, and family. We could hold on to the dreams of the future and have a good deal of hope in what was to come. We would face the fun times and the difficult times together. We would walk hand in hand and as we aged we would look forward to those golden years, the so-called "sunset of our lives".

This scenario holds true even for those women who also work outside the home. Being an employer or an employee does not keep us from fulfilling our God-given role as wife and mother. It does, however, add many extra burdens to our already full lives.

We were not prepared for separation. Whether by death, divorce, or desertion, we were not expecting that turn of events. We have not been equipped to manage life alone. When we have successfully cleaved one to the other, we become overwhelmed by the trauma of our new situation. After our many years of togetherness we are assaulted by the pain brought forth by separation and singleness.

In the beginning we look to God for direction. Sometimes the sky overhead seems like brass and we hear no encouraging words. We wander in the valley of tears, often without direction. We feel lost and emotionally undone.

We struggle for identity. Giving up the right to ourselves at marriage, even to the right to our names. We are no longer known as the child of our parents. We become known as the wife of our husband. Then we become known as the mother of our children. But who are we really?

Until I was able to clearly discern my own identity, I was lost in role playing. I could not seem to see who I was. It was under the painful scrutiny of the Holy Spirit that I was finally able to uncover myself. The uncovering brought me into a closer relationship with God. Through His ministry and the countless unique experiences which He prepared for me, I finally was able to become whom He wanted me to be, in Christ Jesus.

The "single world" is a hard place, filled with shocks and surprises. As the new widow walks through the mine-fields of "the firsts," we come under constant assault. Who would have thought that the simple act of shopping could be so difficult? Probably never before have we considered buying groceries for one person with packages designed for two or more. The grocery cart itself is designed to hold a young one and if we shop in the evening we will often see young couples holding hands, shopping together. Everything seems designed and engineered for two or more, and with sadness our singleness is rudely brought home again, and again.

Trouble is an ever favorite tool of the enemy. It comes to us in power and with regularity. Trouble is always lurking just around the corner, prepared to pounce on us and drag us away with it. It hopes to leave us in an abyss filled with fear, confusion and overwhelming pain.

We must learn not to fear the telephone, the official-looking letter, or the evil report. We learn to look behind, under and around the many boulders which block our path. We come to realize that God cannot show us His power unless there is something that needs over-powering.

Helplessness overwhelms us often, especially when our children are in trouble. Never before have I so appreciated the trials faced by women who are single parents. When trouble confronts our children or our grandchildren, we really don't feel equal to the battle. We feel the lack of our partner in life and our partner in prayer. We have difficulty functioning as a single parent. Somehow our children's problems loom even larger without our husband and their father nearby.

Unless we are blessed with generous friends and neighbors, we will face each household chore, alone. Everything from reconciling the checkbook, paying all the bills, remembering the antifreeze for the car radiator and learning how to put air in the car tires. All of these things move into our work column. These become our responsibility and all too often we are forced to attend to them, alone. Women of my generation are usually ill-equipped.

Much of the damage done to our society by the enemy does not really touch us until we are forced to face single living. Our society has allowed a few to affect life for the many, leaving us with a people that are fragmented and devoid of most moral precepts. As some in our society have tried to move us into the Post-Christian era, we notice that the old standards have fallen to a precarious low. So when we are forced to deal with the institutions that have been set in place to govern us, protect us and give us order, we often come face to face with the uglier side of humanity.

God's rules deal harshly with those who would take advantage of widows. In Deuteronomy 27:19, God says, *"Cursed be he that perverteth the judgment of the stranger, fatherless, and widow. And all the people shall say, Amen."* But the evening news is full of stories about widows being stripped of everything when they foolishly put their trust in lawyers, bankers and even Church leaders.

God's word is clear, the widow is protected by Him. If she will allow God to take that role in her life, then He will extend His arm to protect her. As we learn to come under His authority and live in the precious order of God, we can then live in victory and our composure will show forth His love. On the other hand, if we fight against Him and His Plan, we will then live on the ragged edge, constantly being bombarded by a society which has lost its way. We are under attack daily but the choice about weathering the storm is ours.

We once yielded in marriage to our husbands; now is the time to yield to God. Little by little we let go of our beloved husbands. Every hope, every dream, every unfulfilled expectation, we let them go to God. It is a difficult job, filled with pain and grief. Every day we find a new place to release some of what he meant to us. Pain-filled memories are put into God's hands. We let go of all the roles which we filled for our husband and those which he filled for us. As God leads us, we empty ourselves of all which once was, because he that is dead is our husband no more.

God wants to be our husband. As our thinking begins to change, our position with God changes. We begin to understand death as God's blessing for our mates. We stop thinking about our own loss as grievous and look upon it as God's Perfect Plan. His Plan intended for good. Our attitudes can then change and we become more willing to let go.

Every facet of our relationship must go. We let go physically at the time of death for God has taken our husband from us. But unfortunately we either hold tight to much of the past or we take back that which we have released to Him. God waits to give us a new life. He will not give us the new until we have divested ourselves of the old. However long it takes determines the length of time that we will wear "widow's weeds".

Jesus said, in Matthew 22:29, in a discourse about the hereafter, that we are mistaken because we don't understand the scriptures. In the next verse He said, "Jesus answered and said unto them, Ye do err, not knowing the scriptures, nor the power of God." It will not be as we have been told by those who do not understand the scriptures. We will not be joined together as married couples with our departed loved ones. That is one of the reasons that it is so important to live a good and full life with our mate before death. We won't be offered that opportunity again. Once in Heaven we will all be the same. God's children, married to Jesus, under the Parental and watchful Eye of our God and Father.

In my life, I learned to trust God. The situations that I found myself in were so formidable that I had no other choice. God became my Father when I was Born Again and His Spirit flooded my spirit. I learned to rely on Him as friend and confidant. The more severe the testing, the closer He became. There was no way to think myself out of the troubles which surrounded me. My situation forced me to be obedient to God. In obedience, discernment came. It was an awesome truth of God and I learned it the hard way.

At Bill's death my life was so shaken that I didn't know where God was. I knew that He was "there", but I didn't know where that was. His role in my life changed, as my situation changed. And as I became more willing to change, He became ever so much more to me. And if I would allow Him, He will become even more than I could imagine.

Do I still miss Bill? Yes, and there are still very hard times. After all, I had chosen to spend my whole life with him. Circumstances beyond my control now force me to live without him. Because he was my human companion, I miss him. Never to hear his voice or feel his touch fills me with sorrow. But the grief which once was so brutally piercing has been tamed and has become an emotion which can go as quickly as it comes.

I have learned to live with God as my cover, and in that my life has developed a new richness. I'm beginning to be settled in my relationship with Him. A new kind of comfort blankets me in times of prayer. It has not been easy but it has been accomplished. I have learned to love God with a new love and in a new way.

For the largest part of my life Bill was my husband. Now, he is not my husband. He is free of me. He lives a life untouched by me, a life that I really cannot understand. He let go of me when he died and he took hold of God. I have been letting go of him ever since. In every part of my life as I let go of Bill, God has rushed in to give me comfort. If I became willing, then He would stay. Day by day, I have walked this out. As I have allowed God, He has taken over every role which was once filled by Bill.

God is now my Husband, He is my Provider, my Guide, my Spiritual Head. He is the Lover of my soul and God stands with me. He is ready to act as Protector and Friend, Confidant and Listener as He hears my deepest thoughts. He is my Physician, my Encourager, and my Comrade. He is all that is good for me and He is truly all that I need as husband. Every facet of God is, of course, available to us all.

• • •

There will be some who read this book who are like widows, in the truest sense of the word. They are those whose husbands have divorced or abandoned them, for whatever reason. These women have been left defenseless and broken. God will fill the role as husband for you, also. For if your husband, a believer with no Biblical excuse, has left you cast adrift in this terrible sea, then he has foolishly stepped out of God's will and His perfect order. Always remember that your husband is really in more trouble than you are. When you are left uncovered by the priest of your household, look up because your redemption is nigh. God stands ready to fill every void. As He has done for me, He will do for you. Have no doubt and call upon Him. Be ready for Him to move on your behalf.

For those who still grieve, I say it's OK to grieve, but remember that there is hope for you. Don't allow yourself to be hemmed in by the constraints of conventional wisdom concerning grief. Keep in mind that it is for a season. If you will be obedient to God, call upon Him, rely upon Him, He will carry you through your time of grieving. God is Sovereign and He loves you. He knows your condition and He stands ready to share your grief. It is His desire to remove those burdens from your heart.

Read as I have, Ecclesiastes 3:1-8. Come to understand more about your God and His Perfect Plan for you.

Ecclesiastes 3:1-8 *"To every thing there is a season, and a time to every purpose under the heaven: A time to be born, and a time to die; a time to plant, and a time to pluck up that which is planted; A time to kill, and a time to heal; a time to break down, and a time to build up; A time to weep, and a time to laugh; a time to mourn, and a time to dance; A time to cast away stones, and a time to gather stones together; a time to embrace, and a time to refrain from embracing; A time to get, and a time to lose; a time to keep, and a time to cast away; A time to rend, and a time to sew; a time to keep silence, and a time to speak; A time to love, and a time to hate; a time of war, and a time of peace."*

I pray that this little book has been of help to you and I pray God's richest blessings upon you all. Amen.

Addendum

This book was primarily concerned with the first two years after Bill's death...from the time of the day of his death to my time at Marco Island. Since then the Lord has faithfully maintained His cover and protection over me.

I labored without Bill for seven years at *...in the Name of Jesus Ministries*. During the early part of the seventh year the Lord told me that I would be leaving Cocoa Beach where I had lived for 40 years.

I was to turn the work over to a young man who had been saved and taught under our tutelage. His name is Marc Ivanchack and he received from my hand the building and the contents, with all bills paid. Hallelujah! The Ministry of *... in the Name of Jesus* was to close, but in its place would be WEGO Ministries, a ministry with its eyes on the world. Also God miraculously opened the doors for me to sell the ranch property that Bill and I had loved so much. So on New Years Eve 1998 I left Cocoa Beach and moved to Winter Park, Florida.

Six weeks after Bill's death when I moved from our home to Aunt Gerry's, I had put my furniture in storage. I had asked Him if I should give my furniture away, sell it, or just let it go. I really didn't know what He wanted of me at that time. I was willing to do anything He asked. I stood at the door of the storage facility and heard the Lord say, "Trust me with all of this and I will give you a proper home."

I now live in that proper home. It is more than I could have anticipated or hoped for. God is so gracious. Again I say, trust Him with everything and He shall see you through whatsoever comes. Today He is still my husband and I am well pleased.

To contact the author directly, she can be reached at the address below:

Jane C. Wittbold
690 Osceola Avenue
Unit 502
Winter Park, Florida 32789
jwittbold@cfl.rr.com

Suggested Checklist

This list might vary considering your particular situation but it will give you a general idea of the work ahead. I hope it will help. Don't be afraid, God will help you through it all:

1. Before you leave the hospital you will be asked about your choice of a funeral home. This will be an important decision. If you are in doubt take some time to look into some nearby facilities and ask friends who have had experiences with the funeral homes in your area. Ask questions about costs, reliability and reputation. Don't be pushed into a quick decision. A good funeral home can be a real blessing for the time ahead.

2. Notify your lawyer and accountant. Your lawyer should have a copy of your husband's will and he or she will give you any special information that you will need. Later when you feel a little better you will need to write a new will because your situation has changed. Your accountant will be knowledgeable about your husband's financial situation so he can be a big help to you in this area. Whenever possible they will work together to keep you informed.

3. If your husband received Social Security benefits, then that office needs to be notified quickly. This job will be done for you by any good funeral home. They will also notify the newspapers for the legal obituary. You may dictate to

them any personal requests for the obituary at this time. They are experienced in these jobs and they don't have your emotional involvement, so take advantage of all that they have to offer. After all, you're paying for it. Don't be afraid to ask questions, that's the way you will learn.

4. If you are 60 or over, then you must make contact with the local Social Security office in order to set up your own Social Security survivor's benefits. If you were well employed for a number of years you might be using your own Social Security. The funeral home will help you with telephone numbers and addresses. You may be required to provide proof of Marriage, W2 forms and of course a Death Certificate. If your husband worked for Civil Service then you must notify them. If your husband worked for the railroad you will need to inform the Railroad Retirement Board. The funeral home will be able to advise you on how to get in touch with the agencies that you need. Most of them will have local offices or National 800 numbers.

5. You will need to buy copies of your husband's death certificate. In most cases the funeral home will get these for you. Just be sure to get enough copies. There will be a nominal payment, usually about $6.00 per copy. You will need a few Certified Death Certificates and also some copies. It seems as if everyone in your immediate future will need at least one copy of something. All legal transactions, all mortgage holders, all banks etc. will want a death certificate. Some agencies will need a Certified Death Certificate. Some will be satisfied with a copy. Some will want a Sanitized Death

Certificate, which is one where no cause of death is listed. You can get these at your local Health Department. You will be amazed at the number you need. Of course the more you owned jointly, the more you will need.

6. Notify all Insurance Companies, Retirement Plans and Pension Funds. In recent years many of these companies have changed their names for one reason or another. If you cannot locate the company and your agent is unable to help you, there is a National Insurance Consumer Help Line, 1-800-942-4242. When you make contact with your husband's Insurance Company they will ask for proof of your claim. Send them a copy of his policy. Never send the original policy, even if they ask for it, until you have received their check.

7. If your husband served his country in the military and kept his V.A. benefits active you will need to check with the Veterans Administration in your area or call 1-800-827-1000. He may also be eligible for a burial allowance, flag, or marker. Funeral homes will also supply a flag which can be used at the funeral or memorial service. This flag is yours to keep as a remembrance.

8. Stay in touch with those who can help you. Eat properly and try to get some rest. Don't pull the covers over your head and hope to die. Remember, ask questions and trust God.

9. Other people will also be impacted by your beloved husband's departing and you need to keep up with

answering all the calls, bereavement cards and letters. The funeral home will have a nice selection of acknowledgement cards or you may wish to buy them elsewhere. Remember you have a lot to go through so make it as easy on yourself as possible.

10. Notify your banker in order to change all jointly-held accounts and certificates of deposit. A good banker will show you what these changes will mean to you in the future. Remember, ask questions.

11. Notify your stockbroker and they will help you change ownership of any jointly-held or solely-owned stocks. Be sure to have them cancel any "open" orders arranged by your husband. Check into your IRA and retirement accounts. Transfer any bonds into your ownership. Your stockbrokers can be a great help through this time. They had better treat you well if they want your continued business. Keep in mind that though you don't feel like you are in charge, you are legally. With God's help you will safely move through this troubled time.

12. To transfer all real estate into your sole ownership you must file a Certified Sanitized Death Certificate at the County Courthouse. You might need witnesses. There will be a nominal charge for this. The Courthouse clerks will carefully lead you through the labyrinth of paperwork needed to transfer the property.

13. Notify the Department of Motor Vehicles to transfer Titles of all registered vehicles, mobile homes and/or

boats. There will be a fee for this transfer. If you are going to give your husband's car away you will also have to make this transfer into the name of the recipient. The clerk will advise you if additional documents are needed along with the Death Certificate, the Title and the Registration. You will need proof that you are legally able to transfer the Title. Your lawyer can make those arrangements.

14. You will need to notify all your husband's credit card companies. I got into rough water when I innocently continued to use my card. The card had my name on it, but the account was in the name of my husband. A very rude young man brought me to task insisting that I destroy the card and send the pieces to him immediately. He was so arrogant and showed little compassion for my situation. I was hurt and offended but I did some of what he asked. I did cut up the card but I did not send him the pieces. After this I quickly went about the business of getting credit cards in my own name. Every woman should have her own credit card account so that this sort of thing could not happen. Take advantage of your relationship with your bank, or respond to some of the many cards that come uninvited in the mail. Get yourself enough cards to meet every emergency, depending on your finances, but use them sparingly and keep them paid. If you must keep a balance for a time, pay it off is quickly as possible. Remember you are trying to get a good credit rating so you must use the cards. Always keep in mind that you are responsible for your spending.

15. You need to cancel your husband's Voter Registration and Driver's License. A call to the Courthouse should be enough.

This is not a complete list but it is enough to get you started. It is difficult to include any more details because each life situation is different. I can make no guarantees except for the most important one. God will be faithful and He will see you through this terrible time and increase your wisdom and knowledge of Him with every step. Remember, He loves you!

About the Designer

Kathleen Schubitz, owner and founder of RPJ & Company, Inc. began publishing Christian books in 2004.

Knowing the Lord had given her clear direction for the establishment of the company, including the name taken from Romans 14:17, she set out to bless pastors, leaders, ministers, missionaries and others by offering to publish work to help the Body of Christ. As a designer, poet, author, and speaker, she brings unique experience to the task of publishing.

Whether working on a book, calendar, business card, bookmark or brochure, her workmanship has blossomed in the last year, particularly in the poetry book genre. With her clientele growing rapidly she now has more than 25 published titles in her portfolio.

"I count it an honor and privilege to work with so many talented authors and artists throughout the world. What a blessing to offer them more than their published book, but a special creation designed with each author in mind," she stated recently.

In addition to her publishing efforts, Kathleen Schubitz is the author of *...In His Presence, Finding Purpose after Abuse, Scripture Keys for Finding Purpose after Abuse*, and *Journal to Freedom*.

Learn more about options of publishing your work with Kathleen Schubitz by visiting www.rpjandco.com.

ABOUT THE AUTHOR

Jane Crosbie Wittbold was born in Canada, raised in South America, and returned to Canada to finish her secondary school education. She then moved to Florida to attend Rollins College, whereupon she met and married William John Wittbold. They lived together for many happy years, giving life to a daughter, Katherine, and a son named John. Life was good until the dark hand of alcohol took its toll upon them all. It was at her lowest point that she met God and soon led her husband as well into God's Kingdom.

When the time was right Jane and Bill opened *...in the Name of Jesus Ministries* in Cocoa Beach, Florida. The power of God was present to heal, deliver and set the captives free. They worked together for seven years and Jane continued for another seven after Bill's departure for heaven. It was soon after becoming a widow that Jane visited with Dr. James Wesley Smith, of La Grange, Georgia. He had heard the instructions of the Lord to prepare her for ordination. It was arranged by men but directed and completed by the Holy Spirit.

She now lives in Winter Park, Florida, and attends Calvary Assembly Church. Her life is full and happy while Jesus still holds His role as husband in her life.

CPSIA information can be obtained at www.ICGtesting.com
Printed in the USA
238029LV00002B/8/P